Facebook Advertising:

A Step-By-Step Guide to Profitable Facebook Marketing & Effective Ad Campaigns

By James Moore

Table of Contents

Introduction

For the last few years you have debated about establishing your company. You've worked in retail for 10 years and watched thousands of people walk out of the clothing store because of the prices. You talked to dozens of customers who stated they would support a second-hand thrift store. In fact, the more you talk about this store, the more excited your customers become as they could afford the prices. "Everyone wants to be able to buy a new shirt or pants," one of your customers tell you. After thinking about this comment and realizing this isn't an option for everyone in your city because of the high prices at the current store, you decide to establish a thrift store in your community.

You already have a good sense of your target audience because of your previous experience. But you still take time to conduct thorough research and send out questionnaires. You research the best location for your thrift store, establish your business according to state law, and develop a business plan. After about a year, you are in your new building with a plan to open the doors within a couple of months. You are just missing one main factor and that's your social media advertising. You know Facebook will help grow your business, but you are unsure of the steps in this process.

The contents of this book are here to help you learn how to grow your business with Facebook. From the first chapter to the last, you will learn the steps and tips that will make your business shine and pull people into your business with Facebook advertising. You will discover the importance of a target audience creating your ideal customer. You will learn the importance of focusing on the needs of your customers when creating a profitable marketing campaign. This book will give you the steps to various Facebook advertising strategies and keeping your customers engaged. You will be able to create a marketing campaign that will help you increase sales, brand awareness, engagement, and social recruiting.

Grow with Facebook Advertising: A Step-By-Step Guide to Profitable Facebook Marketing & Effective Ad Campaigns will help you launch your business in the social media world. Over the last decade, Facebook has developed business and community pages specifically for people like you. Through the contents of this book, you will learn how to create powerful Facebook ads that are going to carry your business far into the future. As you continue to learn, you will discover more about yourself and your customers. By keeping an open mind, you will be able to learn more than you thought possible. Whether you have used Facebook before or not, this book is written in a way that you can follow to reach your full potential in the Facebook marketing world.

Chapter 1: How to Grow Your Business with Facebook Advertising

Social network websites take up more than 20% of all online advertisements. This information tells us just how much social media advertising has grown in popularity over the years. Businesses worldwide are recognizing the potential that social media has to grow their business. Social media advertising helps you grow your business in numerous ways such as:

- delivering your advertisements directly in front of the targeted audience;

- enabling tracking and reviewing the consumer's behaviors on all stages of their journey from engagement to conversion;

- consistent insights into the online activities and behaviors of your consumer base that are relevant to your business and brand; and

- consistent media to reach and communicate with your consumers

The nature of social media networks like Facebook allows businesses to gain fast and efficient information on consumer needs and preferences, which are otherwise the data they would only be able to acquire through costly research and extensive surveys.

But not everyone is equally effective with Facebook advertising. Many businesses fail to create effective marketing campaigns, which results in major budget losses. The businesses who don't find success fail to understand and apply the most important strategies and principles of social media advertising, which will be explained in more elaborate detail in the later chapters of this book. For starters, you must understand that the main requirements for effective social network advertising are:

- advertisement content and website links that are relevant and beneficial to the targeted audience, and

- valuable pieces of information that you can easily incorporate into your current marketing strategy.

Advertising on Facebook is done through the network's on-site application, the Ads Manager, which all users can use to design their own advertising campaigns and post the advertisements to the website.

Once you create your Facebook ads, you can then target your ideal audience by location, gender, age, online activities and behaviors, relationship status, job title, college or workplace. Once you select your target audience, Facebook will show you the exact number of potential ad viewers.

Why Are Facebook Ads Helpful in Growing Your Business?

Facebook ads carry the potential for business growth because the users interact with the advertisement the same way they interact with other Facebook users. They can "Like" or "Share" the ad, and they can also participate in the discussion in the comment section. When the viewers of your ad are actively discussing its content, your advertisement will appear on the pages of their "Friends", further spreading the word about your business and your message.

Facebook's Ads Manager provides you with extensive reports on how your ads are performing. These reports also contain information on the click-through rate, or the number of clicks that the ads have received, as well as the breakdown of the viewer's activities and the activities of their contacts related to the advertisement. The network will deliver reports that speak about the efficiency of your campaign, which allows you to track progress. One of the most telling pieces of information is the number of clicks that is calculated based on the amount of time the users have clicked the ad and landed on the advertising page, Liked a page, or RSVP'd to an event that you've been advertising.

How Are You Paying for Facebook Advertising?

There are a couple of ways in which the network charges you for the ad placement. CPC, or cost-per-click, is a unit that measures the charge of a single click or interaction with your ad. CPC also includes Likes, Shares, and Comments, covering all of the activities of your audience on the paid post. You can choose whether or not to set a budget for the ad. If you set a fixed budget, your card will be charged the maximum set amount, and the network will run your campaign until the cost reaches the maximum budget amount. If you don't limit your advertising budget, the network will run your campaign until the funds on your credit or debit card are exhausted.

Aside from setting the overall campaign budget, you can also set a daily budget for your campaign. The daily budget is the limit you will spend on each individual ad and ad set each day. If you set a daily budget limit, the network will run your ads until it reaches the set amount.

What Is a Facebook Marketing Campaign?

A Facebook marketing campaign is a group of ads that you create based on your overall marketing strategy and advertising goals. When designed and planned strategically, Facebook ads will benefit your business because they allow you to group them and segment the audience, sending your message to the most receptive viewer group.

Every Facebook user can create their own advertising campaign. To create a Facebook advertising campaign, you have to have a Facebook profile. You have to have your own profile page, and you can create your advertisement by clicking the "Add Advert" link. There you will fill out a page and complete the details of the advert that you are trying to make. The design of the ad also includes a link to the target destination. The ad needs to contain a title, a body, and the text that describes the ad. You need to choose an image that will be appropriate for the ad, like a business logo, an image of the product, or another image of your choice.

Ad Targeting

Facebook focuses its strategy on the enormous number of its members and leverages this number to offer advertisers the possibility of focused targeting from a broad demographic. Unlike other advertising platforms, the Facebook Ads Manager carries an advantage in terms of giving you the opportunity to select the audience that will view your ad. This way, you have the ability to not only design the ad to cater to your target audience but to also control who will view your ad, meaning that your budget will be spent only on viewers you find desirable for your campaign.

Facebook allows targeting based on demographic profiles and interests that users reveal on their pages. The chances of having a cost-friendly campaign increase with a variety of targeting options. Well-optimized targeting can make a true difference in terms of driving traffic to your website. Sophisticated targeting is all about making sure that your target consumer gives attention to your advertisement. While there's a limit to the amount of data you can collect about prospective consumers, leveraging the available ones in the smartest way is still an option many businesses use to their greatest advantage. Your goal is for your campaign to target those consumers who are most likely to interact with it.

Click-through rates increase when the advertisements are customized by criteria like location, content visited, or the information searched on search engines. While consumers like relevance, they are easily annoyed. If the ads are tailored to their interests and are relevant, consumers are more likely to interact. The effectiveness of the ad depends on the type of profile information that is being used. Demographics, gender preferences, location, and interests have the most important role.

After defining the goal of your marketing campaign, your next step is to define your target audience. The Facebook Ads Manager allows you to choose the viewers of your ad by parameters such as the location, demographics, age, gender, likes, and interests.

Aside from basic targeting, you can also use the advance demographic settings, which include birthday, relationship status, gender interest, languages, education, and work.

How to Manage the Advertising Budget

Facebook gives you plenty of tools to plan and manage your advertising budget.

Setting Up Pricing and Schedule

To run your advertising campaign, you will need to complete the account currency, the time zone, the campaign budget, the ad schedule, and the pricing. Upon completing these steps, you can review your campaign and make any additional desired changes before placing an advertisement order. Having full control of your spending is another benefit to advertising with Facebook. For example, if you paid for a TV or newspaper ad placement, you would have no control over the delivery and efficiency of your ads. On the other hand, Facebook allows you to go back, review your campaign, and make all the necessary adjustments to both keep your ads and audience effective while also controlling your costs.

Create a Community of Supporters

As a business, you can create group pages where your followers don't have to accept you as a "Friend". Instead, the user can simply click "Become a fan" or "Like". Once you publish a Facebook post, it will appear on all of the members' pages. The fan will continue to receive updates from your page unless they "Unlike" your page.

Free Visibility and Referrals

Another advantage of this method of advertising is that your fans' interactions with the page are also visible on their friends' pages. Every time your fan makes an interaction with the page, it will appear on their friend's homepage. This way, you can share both your company information as well as photos, videos, applications, comments, and messages for free.

An Identity Behind the Brand

A Facebook page reveals the identity behind your business to potential customers. This way, your consumer base gets to view you as a personable, human entity instead of an anonymous business that's presented with the other advertising formats. When you build up your business page and form a consistent relationship with the audience, your consumers know what they can expect from your business. This will help them build up trust and secure a friendly relationship with your business.

Why Do You Need a Marketing Strategy?

A marketing strategy is vital for Facebook advertising. A marketing strategy defines:

- what are you trying to achieve with your campaign;
- how to get there; and
- which consumers to target.

To start with, it is essential for you to define a campaign goal. You will base your entire marketing strategy on this goal. Your entire campaign concept needs to revolve around the target audience and their features, particularly when creating the ad description, content, and visuals.

Challenges of Advertising on Facebook

Saturation

While social media advertising remains the most budget-friendly and the best-optimized form of advertising, the saturation of the platform poses a challenge. Your potential user can interact with as many businesses as they want, as well as their contacts. Since it's impossible for Facebook to provide the same level of exposure for everyone, there are different priorities (and algorithms) being applied to secure prioritizing according to the user's interest.

Competition, Recognition, and Relevance

Due to the saturation of the platform, as well as the immense amount of competition, becoming recognized is a challenge. More than that, staying relevant on the platform will require continuous work considering the billions of posts that are being published every single day. Becoming recognized and staying relevant on the platform will require the application of an intelligent strategy.

Create a Community and Increase Engagement

Create a Community Page

When Facebook first launched their community page, they wanted to focus on nonbusiness topics. Facebook CEO Mark Zuckerberg and his team felt they needed to differentiate official business pages from nonbusiness pages, such as fan pages. Unfortunately, this created a lot of confusion and misunderstanding with community pages. An example of a community page is cooking, cleaning, and gardening. The information on community pages is easily found on the internet. However, Facebook users who share an interest in cooking or gardening can connect with each other through the community page.

Over the last few years, a lot has changed with community pages. First, they have become more business friendly. At first, many businesses were frustrated with their community pages because they had no control over them. While people can still create a community page for your business, you are also able to create your own. You can do this as you set up your official business page.

There are three main reasons you want to investigate creating a community page for your business. First, you will have control over the page. Second, community pages are less official than an official business page. This gives you another avenue to understand your audience, which can help you with your marketing strategy. Third, people will share information that they aren't comfortable sharing on an official page.

To create a community page:

1. Go to https://www.facebook.com/pages/creation/ and click the "get started" button under the "Community of Public Figure" option.

2. Enter the type of community and page name.

3. Upload a profile picture and cover photo. If you are creating a community page for your business, you can upload pictures of your building, logo, or a group photograph of your employees.

4. Write your business information in the "About" section. Make sure you take time to edit the information.

5. Ensure that all your information is on the community page, such as business hours, location, contact, and any other information.

6. Share your page with your Facebook friends.

Increase Engagement

One way to know people are noticing your business is through Facebook. When you set up an official business page, you will receive statistical information. For example, you will learn how many people like your page on a weekly basis, like your posts, saw your posts, and clicked any links. To help you notice your business's progress, it's a good idea to keep track of this information. You can do this through Facebook or by recording the information.

Like most people, you will be glued to the amount of attention your posts receive, especially when you are starting. Don't become discouraged if you feel people aren't paying attention to your page. It takes time to build a business and increase engagement. Instead of slowly watching the numbers increase, incorporate some of these tips to help boost engagement.

1. Create posts where people need to answer a question. Don't make it a complicated question. Ask them something that pertains to your business. For example, if you have a flower shop, you can ask them "What is your favorite flower?" You can also ask them a question where they have to fill in the blank. For

instance, "A _____ flower follows the sun." You could allow them to guess for fun or have a contest where the first correct response receives a prize.

2. Give an inside look into your company. You can do this by taking photographs of your lobby, office, or your employees.

3. If you notice one of your fans shared something relevant to your business, share it on your page. This can make someone feel special and also help start a conversation.

4. Give your fans a reason to smile. Do something special for the people who are following your page. This could be anything from a quote that's relevant to your business to having a customer appreciation day. You also don't need to be serious all the time. If you come across a joke that's relevant, post it. Laughing is a way to keep people engaged.

5. Pay attention to what posts are liked more. You might notice a trend with the time frame or what type of content you are posting.

6. Use images as much as possible. People often stop scrolling to look at images and are more likely to engage.

Become Personable & Accessible

Customer service is one of the most important characteristics of a company. Whether you are conversing with a customer face-to-face, over the phone, or online you want to be personable. This can often be overlooked through Facebook because you don't have to worry about your facial expressions, voice tone, and body language. You do need to pay attention to the words and phrases you use, your punctuation, spelling, and written tone.

No matter how you converse, you always need to be respectful. This is often easy to do when people leave good reviews or comments. Unfortunately, not every review or comment you receive will be positive. It's easy to respond negatively after reading a rude comment. You want to do what you can to respond politely and respectfully even when a customer does not. Think of it this way – everyone who visits that post can read the comments. They will read the upset customer's comment and yours. How you respond is going to reflect on your business.

Accessibility is another way to be personable and gain followers. People use Facebook for a variety of reasons. For example, they might be searching for the nearest flower shop when they come across your page. They would like to order a certain flower but aren't sure if you have it in stock, so they send you a direct message. Responding to that message as soon as possible is going to benefit your company. In fact, it could help you make a sale.

Learn Customer Needs & Preferences

You need to get to know your customers so you can learn how your business can benefit them. When people are going to pay to use a service, they want to make sure there is something that will help them. For example, you are promoting your new product on your Facebook page, but it's not generating engagements. You look at the post and notice it simply describes the product. There is nothing that helps connect the product to your customer. You then create a new Facebook post about the product that focuses on how it will benefit the customer. This post is going to generate more interest because you have focused on your customer's needs.

Optimize your Landing Page

If you're designing an ad that links to your website, be it a blog or a shopping page, optimizing that page to align with the campaign has a major role in generating conversions. One of the ways to make your Facebook advertising campaign more effective is to align your landing page with your ad in terms of style, tone, content, and esthetics.

Keyword Research and Context

While keyword research is a useful part of the targeting, it is not the method that speaks the most about customer needs and preferences. While keyword research may reveal the topics that the users are most interested in, it can't reveal the intention and circumstances surrounding these searches. Keyword research, while useful, lacks context. To uncover the issues surrounding the search interest and the intention, you can try to research the questions that the audience is asking that are relevant to your industry. There are numerous websites that focus on answering an indefinite number of questions. The great news is that all of these websites are free to use. You can use them to not only research the customer pain points but also answer the questions yourself, giving educated advice from an expert point of view.

Finding out what bothers your customers by reading the top-rated and most popular questions within your industry is a lot more informative and time effective than running keyword research and analyzing the extensive amounts of information. By reading and answering the burning questions relevant to your industry and consumers, you are both learning about the pain points and building your business's online reputation.

Aside from pain points, researching questions will give you a glimpse into the background, context, and circumstances that the user faces related to the problem, which you can leverage to craft quality content and upscale your posts using storytelling.

Research Feedback

In addition, reading the feedback that the audience gives to the relevant products and services gives you insight into their needs and wants. Consumers leave very honest, blunt, and unbiased feedback. Reading this feedback could tell you about the details that customers care about, but otherwise aren't mentioning. Such details might include shipping and delivery, pet peeves related to the size and shape of the product, as well as minor to major troubles the consumers have when using the product.

Expert Search Engine Optimization (SEO) Tools

While traditional SEO techniques are effective in helping you pinpoint the right audience members, there are a number of other tools that can help you as well. Using keyword analysis software, you can trace the keywords and key phrases that the consumers are searching. You can use these keywords to optimize your content in a way that highlights the exact problems that the customers are researching. SEO tools are particularly effective with PPC campaigns. They can help you identify the right ideas for your content, whether it's a particular ad, your landing page, or the content of your landing page.

Stalk the Competition

By analyzing the discussions on your competitors' pages, you can also track the typical problems that users are having with their products and services, as well as the problems that are driving them to seek the product as a solution.

Create Profitable Marketing Campaigns

Over the last few years, Facebook has helped thousands of businesses grow. Your business can become a part of this list if you put forth the effort and take the steps to generate a large Facebook fan base. Other than the tips we have already discussed, one of the most important methods is ensuring your marketing campaign is generating a profit. Below are some of the most common steps to help you launch a successful marketing campaign.

Step One: Target the Right Audience for Your Business

Whether you are just starting out or have run a successful business for years, you will want to ensure you are always on target with your customers. This means you will conduct surveys which lets them tell you how you're doing. You will also listen, converse, and get to know your customers at an individual level.

You can use some of Facebook's tools, such as the "Detailed Targeting" search engine to find similar pages. Some of your followers might already follow these pages. When you share posts from these targeted pages or follow them, your followers will notice and feel more connected to your business. You will also be able to get ideas for advertising or what to post in order to gain followers.

Step Two: Create Interesting and Eye-Catching Ads

To create ads that will catch the eye, you know to know a few basic facts about the average Facebook reader. First, they spend about a second looking at ads as they are scrolling through their news feed. This means you need to create an ad which is going to catch their eye quickly. Second, the average person reads at an eighth-grade level, so don't create complicated ads with words the general public won't understand. If you don't follow these two points, people are going to skip over your ad.

When you use an image, it should be simple, describe your product or service, and be high quality. People are more likely to look at ads that are colorful and happy. If you are trying to sell a product, it's best to use people who look happy using your product.

Step Three: Create an Interesting Landing Page

A landing page is the place the user comes to after clicking on your ad. This page should be as engaging as your advertisement, website, and Facebook page. You want to ensure you spend a great deal on the product you're selling. You don't need to put a lot of information on your landing page as people will only spend a few seconds looking at it. Therefore, you want to focus more on easy to understand relevant information about your product. You will also want to include a series of high-quality images as they are known to increase sales by 30% (Laja, 2011).

Step Four: Make Sure You Test Your Ads

One of the nice traits about Facebook's business page are the tools you use. One of these tools will allow you to test your ads. The A/B testing tool will help you look at imagery and help you increase profits. The best way to keep track of your testing is to only test one ad or landing page at a time.

Common Mistakes

Just like there are several tips and steps which go into creating profitable Facebook ads, there are also mistakes that can damage your business through your marketing campaign.

Your Audience Is Too Broad

You want to ensure you target a specific audience. However, you also don't want to make it too narrow. At the same time, you don't want to focus on a broad audience. There is a central point when it comes to your audience that can be difficult to find. But, once you secure this point, you will be able to increase your customer base and your sales.

One of the biggest reasons this mistake is made is thinking everyone can become your customer. Take a moment to think about how many stores you won't shop at because you aren't interested. Everyone else is the same way. There are stores they shop at and there are stores they don't. If you have a business that focuses on athletic shoes, your main customer base is going to be athletes. While everyone wears shoes, women who want high heels or dress shoes won't go to an athletic shoe store. In order to gain the best from Facebook's advertising, you need to target your customer base.

You Don't Do Your Research

One of the first steps to creating a target audience is to research. There are several ways you can conduct research from focusing on your statistics from ads, looking at your competition, and surveys. No matter what you do, you need to do a thorough job, keep your findings, and continue to research. Don't get the idea that you only research your target audience when you are starting your business. Some of the most profitable businesses are always performing research focused on their customers. This allows them to keep up to date on what their customers need and want.

When you skip your research, you won't create your ideal customer. This is an idea of your best customer. While your typical customer won't be exactly like your ideal customer, they will have similar characteristics. Through your best customer, you will be able to critically think about your customers' needs. You will be able to create products that will benefit your customers. You will also be able to create better ads as you will have this person in mind no matter what you do.

Not Giving Your Ad Campaign Enough Time

When it comes to your ad campaign, consistency is key. When you create your first few ads, you might feel that you are losing money instead of gaining followers. This will make you feel that you need to change your ads or stop one ad and start a new one.

One of the biggest reasons why you shouldn't do this is because it will affect your results. You wouldn't be able to get a good idea of how many people are engaging in your ads because you don't allow them to run very long. You can miss opportunities when you pause them or take them down because you aren't reaching your engagement goals right away.

A second reason is that you can end up confusing your customers. The people who do engage and like your page can start to struggle to keep up with your information and products. They might feel that your business isn't stable because it's not consistent. They feel that you are changing your advertisements too often which means you are indecisive. This can negatively affect your customer base as they might lose interest in your company.

It is important to have patience, especially when you are launching your first few ads. It always takes time to build a business, no matter how many posts you make, how often you go live, or how many advertisements you have on Facebook.

Chapter 2: Why Do You Need a Facebook Marketing Campaign Plan?

Setting up your social media plan includes thinking through strategies and methods you want to use in order for your marketing efforts to be lucrative. A Facebook marketing plan is a clean and clear overview of all aspects and steps you will take to execute profitable marketing campaigns. You can start planning from a yearly perspective and then specifying quarterly, monthly, and weekly marketing goals and strategies. A strategic approach to marketing starts with defining your goals and then looking for the ideal online customer to deliver your campaign to. Social media is constantly changing, as well as the audience's tastes and preferences. With social media, your approach should be to start small and carefully, analyzing the response of the audience along the way.

If you are new to social media, going into the process without prior research could result in major financial losses. To avoid this, research your competition and the strategies that they are using. Analyze their advertisements, timing, and the characteristics of the content that are appealing to their customers. While your campaign should be authentic, creating a frame of reference in terms of what is effective and what is ineffective is a good guideline.

While researching, make notes and start the process of defining your ideal audience. You can do that by sending out a survey to your current audience members, sending out emails, and finding out where they are most active online.

Next, you want to find out what are the main challenges of your audience. This will help you find ways in which you can contribute to solutions for these problems. Planning this in advance will help you come up with innovative ideas. In general, one of your goals is to map out your ideal client and spend some time thinking about the strategies that you can use to deliver an innovative solution. This is the part of the process in which you'll open up the questions of which features of your products and services you want to highlight, as well as which tone and voice you want to use in order to pass this message. One helpful way to come up with innovative ideas is to try and improve the shortcomings of already successful competitor campaigns. Staying fresh and up to date is important in creating a compelling Facebook advertising campaigns, and the only way to keep up with the advertising trends in the industry is to analyze both your audience and the activity of your competitors. The social media pages and blogs that your users follow give insight into the type of content they are most responsive and receptive to.

What is a Facebook Marketing Campaign Plan?

A Facebook marketing plan, much like any other marketing plan, is a concise breakdown of strategies and steps you will take with executing a successful advertising campaign. Your marketing plan is an on-paper list of the key elements that focus on the most essential points such as:

- Who is your ideal customer?
- What information Your Facebook advertising plan should contain.
- Online locations that your current customers frequently visit.
- The online pages and websites where your competitors most frequently advertise.
- An analysis of your competitors' campaigns that includes a breakdown of the right and wrong approaches to creating and delivering ads.

Create Your Target Audience

The importance of targeting will be thoroughly explained throughout this book. In order to reach the most important audience members, you will focus on identifying the following indicators:

- the pain points that relate to your industry and products;
- innovative and authentic strategies to solve these problems;
- the most popular topics within your industry and the topics that are most relevant to your consumers;
- typical consumer behaviors and activities on social media, as well as other online activities that are relevant to your product or service; and
- other pages, websites, and blogs that your audience follows.

With this in mind, you will proceed to research both your competitors and the audience base, discovering strategies that will be the most appropriate for your campaign goals.

Defining Goals

Advertising with a goal in mind is essential for both the efficiency of the campaign and budget control. By setting your goals, you will answer the following questions:

- How do you want to grow your business, starting from the point at which you are now?

- How much do you want to increase your sales, leads, and customer base?

After mapping out the long-term goals, which we will elaborate in more detail in the following chapters of this book, you will move on to specify the short-term goals.

Your short-term goals will relate to the long-term goals, but they will be more precise and focused on the exact steps you will take to reach the particular milestones of growth, such as:

- gain more followers monthly;

- increase monthly sales;

- increase subscribers by X%; or

- increase website traffic by X%.

Aside from defining long-term and short-term goals, your marketing plan will include the breakdown of smaller tasks you will do monthly, weekly, and daily, in order to achieve the goals. You will also note the metrics that you want to use for tracking these goals, such as clicks, website visits, the increase in conversions, social media activity, etc.

Based on this, you will create your action list that will refer to exact steps that you will take, such as researching and analyzing data, designing and creating ads, as well as tracking the efficiency of these ads (analyzing your click-through rate, impressions, and the activity on your ads). You will also analyze the success of your campaign by tracking the increase in the number of followers and visitors to your website.

Content plan

In terms of advertising, the content plan relates to the design and strategies you will use to create effective ads. Your marketing plan will contain the drafts of your lead magnets, content plan, strategies, and ideas, as well as the schedule of your marketing campaign.

Content organization and planning is one of the biggest focus points, next to targeting, when creating a Facebook advertising campaign. Your content strategy should contain a detailed overview of the following:

- **Yearly content plan.** Your yearly content plan will define the topics you will cover on a yearly level, as well as the content of your ads and posts that will align with the general plan and the overall campaign goal.

- **Tone and voice.** You will base the tone and voice of your content on your brand values, as well as consumer characteristics and needs.

- **Visuals and calls-to-action.** Your marketing plan will also contain a plan of visuals that you'll be using for your posts and advertisements.

Benefits of a Facebook Marketing Plan?

Now that you understand what a Facebook marketing plan is and how to create one, you should know what you will gain.

It Will Help You Keep Your Audience Engaged

Once you have pulled your audience into your ads and business page, you need to switch gears to keep them engaged. Because of Facebook's tools, keeping your audience interested isn't difficult, you just need to take the time. For example, one day a week you can go live on Facebook. When you go live, your video ends up at the top of everyone's newsfeed. People can also receive notification when you are live. You can also record videos and use Facebook groups.

You Can Provide Customer Support

Customer support is just as important as customer service. There are several ways to provide support to your customers on Facebook whenever necessary. You can use direct messaging, Facebook groups, and messenger bot. A messenger bot is artificial intelligence which will have a conversation with your customer. Messenger bots are programmed to answer questions and complete tasks. Facebook is constantly working to improve their tools for businesses. For example, they also give businesses a chance to hold community discussions.

Facebook Marketing Has Low Operating Expenses

While you can put money toward generating stronger traffic for your business page, you don't have to spend anything on the content you place on Facebook. You can create your own video ads, go live, create your landing page, and do everything for your business page without giving Facebook a cent. This is extremely helpful for start-up businesses or business which are struggling. Not only can you continue to stay in contact with your customers, but you can engage new customers.

If you do choose you pay to sponsor an ad, you can limit how much money you put toward the ad. You get to choose the number of days, focus on a location, and select any other options available. This will also allow you to get an idea of who is focusing more on your ads. For example, you can break the statistics down by age, gender, and location.

You Can Increase Your Website Traffic

Through your Facebook business page, you can promote your website. This can increase the amount of traffic to your website. If people are interested in your Facebook page, they are going to continue to look into your company. This means you can use your Facebook page strategically. Your page isn't meant to hold all the information that your website will hold. You can lead interested customers toward your website by providing links and discussing how there is a lot more information located on your site.

Chapter 3: How to Set Your Facebook Campaign Goals

Facebook Advertising Goals

Create the Campaign Goals According to Your Needs

Setting the right goals is the first step to a good marketing strategy. You should measure your marketing strategy against different criteria to make sure that your advertising strategy is successful. The first step to creating the right goals is performing detailed research to make sure that you are working on an attainable plan. Some of the most successful marketing goals include:

- increased brand awareness
- increased community engagement
- increased sales and lead generation

In case you haven't yet created your Facebook advertising goals, you can look up survey results and look for overlaps between the statistics and your company's goals that have already been set.

How to Go About your Goals?

Most businesses focus on a couple of growth-boosting goals when creating their social media advertising campaigns. Some of these goals are:

Increase the quality of sales

You can improve the quality of your sales with good targeting. A well-planned marketing strategy ensures that you'll be more efficient in reaching your target audience. A broad demographic to deliver your ads to doesn't always guarantee more conversions. It is the right group of users you are aiming for. You can use Facebook Ad optimization as a good method to improve your reach.

Add Value to Your Business

Drawing information from Facebook can assure a better relationship with your customers, more brand awareness, and better resources for your audience.

Industry Insight

If you want to stand out in such a saturated environment like Facebook, you'll need to study your competition. Luckily, the available information about their interactions with consumers provides sufficient material for marketing research. By applying marketing research across your competitor's campaigns, you can detect the most effective strategies, the most popular issues, and the most common mistakes to watch out for. If your demographic overlaps with that of the competitor, looking into their responses to the others' advertising campaigns will provide a glimpse into what you can expect with your ads. Pay attention to the following:

- satisfaction/dissatisfaction
- mention of purchases/prices
- questions that are being asked or overlooked
- complaints

You can leverage this information to gain the upper hand and prepare to give out the information the customers are interested in but don't seem to have access with other brands/businesses. This is a good way for you to become a good listener and be aware of the industry's dynamic and pace.

Efficient Recruiting

Social media can be an efficient tool in discovering top talent. You can also work with your current employees' social network profiles by supporting brand promoting, which will ensure that more of the talented individuals become aware of the new business opportunities with your company.

Cost-effective Growth

Well-optimized social media campaigns can help you limit spending, reduce churn, and increase acquisition. Ad spend, social selling, and increased targeting all help you reach your targeted consumer base at a reasonable cost. The better you target your consumers, the greater the chances of successful relationships long term.

Goal Tracking

You'll have to make sure that you possess the right tools to track your campaign. Different software helps you look over and analyze your Facebook campaign, balancing the ratios between the impressions, engagements, and clicks. You'll also get to see your ike/unlike ratio, which enables you to compare the spikes in user activity with your most recent posts to detect those that have been drawing versus repelling the audience. This way, you can identify which elements of your content are working FOR your marketing goals versus those that are working AGAINST you.

Increased Sales

Over the years, Facebook has erupted on the social media scene and most people are connected. Because of this, businesses use Facebook in order to keep their customers informed, engage new customers, and boost sales. While Facebook has not always been used for this purpose, the last few years have proven that an increase in sales is one of the social media site's many benefits for businesses.

Every step you take to create interest and draw in more of an audience can help increase sales. For example, business posts are public, which means when one of your followers likes a post, it can show up on their friends' timeline. This can create interest for the friend, who might start following your page and purchase a product.

On average, people spend close to an hour a day scanning their Facebook news feed (Standberry, 2017). Furthermore, ads will often show up on a user's page several times. This can be a benefit for your business because the more people see the same ad, the more interested they become in the ad. They want to know why Facebook keeps leading them to your product. This will cause them to check out your product, Facebook page, and possibly your website.

When you set goals to increase sales, you want to be realistic. It's always a wonderful thought to increase your sales by 100 products or more every week, but this is probably not realistic. You will have weeks where your sales increase and you will have weeks where they decrease. The trick in establishing good sales goals is to focus on why sales increase one week and decrease the next. When you are able to pinpoint certain reasons, you will work these into your marketing plan. This will help you increase sales continuously over time.

It's important to remember that an increase is often slow moving. This means that you might only increase your sales by an average of 10 more products each week. This doesn't mean you should keep your goal at 10 products. Instead, start at 10 and then slowly work your way up. For example, for the first three weeks you are at 10 sales every week. You then increase this number to 12 sales for three weeks. As you continue to find what works best with advertising, you will continue to raise your number of sales every three weeks.

Increase Brand Awareness

There are several ways that you can increase brand awareness in the Facebook world. Some of these ways are hashtags, stories, call to action, and saying more with less.

Hashtags

If you are a part of the social media world, you know what hashtags are. People use #hashtags for everything. The main reason for this is because people who use hashtags generate a tag with that word of phrase. This allows other people to look at what people are saying and doing about this topic. For example, if you are at the Minnesota State Fair, you might post a picture with the caption "#MNStateFair2019." This will allow anyone who uses this tag to show up in the same area with your post.

When hashtags first came out, it was really important to use them in certain circumstances. However, this has changed. Today, people will create their own hashtags for any topic. They write these hashtags in any way and include any combination of numbers and letters. Some people hashtag the way they are feeling while others use hashtags as a way to prove a point.

As a business, the main reason you will use hashtags is to create brand awareness. When people read through the posts about the tag, they will come across your business. They will read your post and then continue to scroll through other posts. People don't often click on certain people or businesses or use the hashtags. Therefore, it is not an effective strategy to increase sales or page members.

While hashtags are a great way to get information across, you don't want to include too many in your post. This can become overwhelming for your viewers. It can also create confusion.

Stories

Another way to increase brand awareness is through stories. These stories can be about how your business developed or from your customers. Stories are a very powerful way to get a person's attention. Similar to videos, you will want to keep your stories short and straight to the point. Some of the most powerful stories come from nonprofits or businesses which are designed to help people. They are stories which reach into their iewers' emotions. For example, if you are selling a skin-care product, your stories will consist of people who state how much your product changed their self-confidence.

People also like stories which are educational in nature. For instance, a customer can discuss how they learned your product was the best to solve their problem. Nevertheless, you don't want to make the story too educational. You need to have a mix of education and entertainment.

Call to Action

A clear call to action will get a lot of people interested in your brand. The key is you want to make a call to action easy and quick. People don't spend a lot of time on one post or website when it comes to social media. When creating a call to action, you want the content to be high quality and compelling. This will keep them reading to your next step, which is what you want them to do. For example, you can tell your viewers that everyone who shares your post is eligible for a drawing.

A second point to remember when requesting a call to action is you want to create the content in a way that aligns with your values. Focus on the point of the advertisement or what you are trying to do. For example, if you want people to share to get the word out about your new service, don't ask them to go to a separate website and download an app.

Saying More with Less

When using social media, the average attention span for an adult is about eight seconds (Beese, 2016). On top of this, customers see dozens of posts a day, which causes them to forget about your advertisement easier. Therefore, the less you say, the better your post will be. However, it is still important to get the point across. This means you have to find a way to say more with less.

Some people will do this by posting a link on the bottom of their post. While this can give them an image to the page they linked, most people aren't going to click on the link unless they are extremely interested. With this said, a link is not the most valuable way to say more with less.

One key factor is to say the most valuable information within the first three to four words. This can be difficult for someone who is new to advertising, but once you have done it a few times you will quickly get the hang of it.

Another key factor is to include visuals that say what you want without words. For example, if you company is running a bicycle sale, your caption could read "Bicycle Sale Now!" with an image of a young child excited about their new bicycle.

Chapter 4: How to Find Your Target Demographic

Facebook Demographic Insights

One of the most beneficial aspects of using Facebook advertising to grow your business is the ability to look into the details of your demographic. You can look into your audience's breakdown and use this information to plan your marketing strategies and methods. Relevant information in terms of consumer demographics includes their locations, language, education levels, income levels, gender, and other pointers. To get to know your consumer demographic better, you can use your Facebook Page insights.

Facebook audience demographics shows you the breakdown of your page fans by age groups, gender, and engagement.

Be the First to Engage

You'll have to take a lead when it comes to creating a connection with your audience on Facebook. Make sure to initiate and ignite discussions, conversations, and content sharing all through the loop of your current marketing idea. For example, you can open up a debate about solving a problem or a situation that involves your product/service. For example, if you're advertising your landscaping services, you can ask you fans which are their preferred styles and whether some are better than others. You can also conclude that summertime is challenging in terms of watering and spark a discussion about the landscape layout that makes watering more efficient.

Never stay silent to discussions being opened up on your page. While you can assume a position that is respectful to all of your fans' viewpoints, you can use these discussions to position yourself as a reputable figure for solving a particular problem. Industry chats and discussions are a great way for you to build up your community. When starting a fresh page, don't forget to be very up-front when asking people to join and announcing your upcoming activities. There are plenty of ways for you to increase engagement, but your initiative will make or break your campaigns.

Geolocation

What does your audience want? When shaping your content, your primary focus should be on the wants and needs of your audience. So, what does the social media audience look for when it comes to content?

Entertainment

Nearly half of audience members respond well to entertaining content. The element of entertainment, viewed either as humor or other ways of sparking interest, makes the audience more likely to engage. When designing your ad content, look for the most engaging content that contains video, images, and memes. Over half of the examined Facebook audience, according to statistics, engages well with ads that include these elements.

Emotion

Content that speaks to emotion is also popular and the audience is more likely to notice and remember it. If your ads appeal to the emotional side, rather than commercial, the audience will be more likely to interact.

In addition, the audience is more likely to engage with the ads that include popular influencers, which can spark an idea for you to look into the possibility of collaborations with other people who are relevant within your niche.

Education

Informative content also ranks high in terms of engagement. Offering beneficial information to your readers that also explains how your brand can help them solve problems and overcome challenges drives engagement. What does this tell you? Make sure that your content is informative and that it relates to the type of information that the audience is interested in. A third of examined audience members confirmed that they are more likely to engage with the brands that are offering interested but beneficial blog posts. Mainly, "actionable" content ranks high, with most important strategies being to offer free downloads or a printable item that provides a form or an instruction to solve some kind of a problem. Users also seek a social experience, which is why they are also more likely to interact with the content that includes them in a learning community. Among other, content pieces that offer instruction in solving problems and those that show readers how certain products can be used in unusual ways also spark more interest.

This type of content offers a high amount of value in the consumers' eyes, which can contribute to cultivating brand loyalty. Over time, your audience will identify that your page is a source of good and useful information and will want to come back for more.

Freebies

Other than simply directing the audience to purchase your product, offering any type of saving, such as a discount or coupon code, also works well with the consumer. They are more likely to engage with the ad if they have a perception of saving, even if that discount isn't that great. This, however, requires segmenting by age groups, since each individual age group shows different content preferences. Some respond better to storytelling, while others prefer entertaining content.

Targeting

Who are you trying to reach with your ad campaign? Prices vary when it comes to ads when observed by the age groups. Make sure to tailor your ads by age group preferences rather than simply applying the same strategy across various different groups.

The Importance of Testing

While you can employ a great amount of effort into targeting and tailoring your demographics, testing is crucial in identifying the most successful strategies and designs. Testing helps find out which ads are the most motivational for your audience to engage, and which ones are more effective in speaking to them directly.

Understanding these specifics of your demographic and creating personalized ad campaigns will set you up for greater success than going in with a blindfold and guessing. For this, the process of consumer research will ensure a more strategic approach and the better distribution of your advertising budget across the entire campaign. As a result, you'll have an audience that views your ads as interesting and beneficial, and they'll also understand that you are viewing them as people rather than an opportunity to sell.

Meticulous budgeting requires a thought-out approach that includes both research and design.

Age and Gender Demographics

Knowing the statistics in terms of Facebook user demographics helps you better target the audience and map out the right consumer for your product.

Age

While roughly the same percentage of men and women use Facebook, it is also popular with 51% of teenagers and 81% of adolescents. When it comes to the age group of 30-49, 78% of them use Facebook. Past this age line, the use of Facebook starts to decrease, with 65% of men and women between the ages of 50-64 and roughly 41% over 65 years of age using the network. What does this information tell you? Mainly, effective social media campaigns are geared toward a younger audience, who is more active online and more likely to search for solutions and shop online. Depending on your industry, you might find yourself in need of adjusting your marketing strategy or even your products and services to cater to a younger audience.

Location

When it comes to location, a vast majority of Facebook users reside in urban areas— 75%, while 67% of them live in suburban areas. Residents of rural areas take up the smaller percentage of Facebook audience at 58%. What does this information tell you? The number of audience members you have at your disposal can significantly impact your targeting options and also your budget. When implementing the geolocation into your ad campaign, make sure to track how choosing certain locations affect the CPC or cost-per-click. If you're running your business locally, your local consumer might be a smaller crowd but able to bring in greater profits than the nonlocal audience. On the other hand, if your business is international, going with certain populations geographically can significantly impact the cost of your campaign. If your goal is conversions, you might have to plan a higher budget for certain populations. On the other hand, if you're starting out and want to build up followers, you can choose the cheaper locations if that population offers a sufficient number of potential viewers for you to meet your goals.

Scheduling Posts and Posting Times

Knowing and understanding how your audience uses Facebook entails knowing the right times to post your ads. Scheduling is a no-brainer. You want to time your ads when the greatest number of your prospects are online. Luckily, statistics are pretty clear about the ideal posting times across different target audiences and industries. You can use this information to create a good posting schedule that will put your ads in front of people who are most likely to interact at the current time.

In general, Wednesday from noon to 1pm is the best time to show your ads. If you want to run an everyday campaign, you can expect success if you time it anywhere between 9 am and 3 pm. You want to avoid showing your ads on Sundays and focus on the midweek periods since these are the times where the users are most active on social media. The ideal posting times can vary across different industries, so aside from researching the general most recommended times to post, also make sure to include the findings that relate to your industry and preferably your location.

Chapter 5: How to Create a Target Audience

How Much Information Do Facebook Users Reveal About Themselves?

While Facebook users can enjoy the website for free, they are required to give out pieces of important information in order to create an account. Their full name and locations, as well as address and phone number, including information about their birth date and gender, are only some of the information that the website gathers on its users. Users also leave traces of information that relate to their education and employment, both current and previous. Relationship status is also available for users to express whether or not they're currently involved in a relationship or if they have a family. Whichever your target demographic is, the information given in their Facebook profile provides a glimpse into their lifestyle and habits.

The demographic largely varies due to the enormous number of Facebook users. Facebook users engage with the platform with the goal of socializing and sharing information about their activities and likes and dislikes. For you it means that you're given a platform from which you can learn a lot about your customers, which is all the information they are willing to give out for free and they're usually more honest than in surveys. This way businesses like you have the opportunity to get a closer look into their customers' lifestyles. Moreover, Facebook users bond around similar interests which helps your ability to structure the demographic based on group memberships and page likes. While you can create pages in the group that consumers can use to interact with your brand, you can also incorporate social media into your current marketing strategies. However, keep in mind that Facebook users have a generally negative attitude toward advertisement. The administrators of the website are constantly working on improving the visibility of advertisements while staying respectful to the wants of the audience who prefer not to be bothered with them. It is a gentle balance which entails frequent changes in algorithms and changes in layouts of the advertisements. How does this apply to you? When designing Facebook marketing strategies, keep in mind to stay in the loop with pending changes and updates that might affect the efficiency of your ads.

On the one hand, creating accurate conclusions based on raw data may seem like a daunting task. On the other hand, looking into the vision that you had for the campaign before the analysis and the concept you had after is a good demonstration of the difference in direction you took to get closer to the consumer.

Your social data can provide a good look into the profile of a social media persona. Social data rounds up the numbers for you and gives the percentages of different customer profiles. This can help you identify not only the best strategies but also the ability to track and adjust along the way. One of the simplest ways to do this is to look into your most effective advertisements and use them as a base to create future campaigns. Knowing the best times to publish (meaning those times when the consumer base is interacting the most) helps with future scheduling and reduces the cost of ineffective timing.

What do nonsocial analytics tell you? Not only the activity on social media but also CRM data, information about shopping and the activity on your website, and Google analytics help you detect the audience's behavior when they're not interacting on social media. This is the type of "what they say versus what they do" relationship that can tell you the real features that are hiding behind proclaimed interests and values. For example, if your consumer base seems to interact with a product of a budget category on social media that is different than the category they are searching for, it might be a hint to you that they have secret interests or pain points that they aren't likely to vocalize. Addressing these issues creates a feeling that your business truly understands their needs. For example, if your millennial group interacts with high-end brands on social media but frequently looks for discounted products, it can be a signal that there is a major gap between their desires and their spending power. What can you do with this information? You can go about it in different directions. For example, you can try to implement the desired elements into your product while keeping it budget friendly, or you can work on discounts and promo codes. Off-social-media activity is a good guide for you to detect needs that aren't being vocalized.

In terms of advertising, you can discover which websites your consumer base visits most frequently and perhaps choose to advertise there as well.

Last, but not least, one of the best ways for you to find out more about your audience is to simply ask more questions. Showing interest in the user's opinions and experiences shows your personable character, and it also shows your desire to directly cater to the user's needs. You can create simple posts but also give a survey or a quiz.

What to Do with Your Social Media Personas?

Having all this information isn't very useful if you don't know how to use it properly. Here are some of the good ways for you to do that:

Segmentation

Your likely conclusion will most likely be that there are multiple subgroups within each recognizable group. After all, people are a colorful group, and all of them having similar interests and needs is close to impossible. To segment your ad campaign, create different ads that target multiple audience segments. It might sound simple, but it also calls for different content design, visuals, and messages across each ad, along with specific timing that has proven most effective for individual students. Some of the more obvious segments would be working versus stay-at-home parents. The small variations in your audience help you segment you campaign and look into all of the relevant details.

What does adapting to multiple audiences do for you? It helps you adapt the tone and voice of your brand to be more personable, creating a much more authentic approach to communicating with the consumers. Adapting your tone to the demographic makes it easier for you to appeal to the audience and convey your message in a more understanding way. This is relevant to determine whether or not to use humor and jokes, symbolism, reference history and tradition, or future and innovation instead. The tone you'll use for your advertising needs to appeal to both taste but also the pain point of the consumer base. More obvious examples are that a quieter, softer tone is appropriate when addressing health concerns, while humor and jokes are more appropriate for the entertainment industry.

On the other hand, there are general demands of positivity across all groups, since consumers don't respond well to negativity regardless of the circumstances.

Social Personas and Content Strategy

Finally, consider how social personas are instrumental to your content strategy. Knowing their needs, wants, and frustrations helps direct the order and the system through which you'll convey your messages and organize your content. Aside from the logical order of the issues you want to address, you can also organize your content around priorities and trends that are currently popular in your audience group. You can strategize around different content types depending on their popularity and suitability for the different topics.

Last, but not least, you'll have to continuously update your knowledge on social media personas to keep up with the fluctuations in their interests, goals, objectives, and needs. Some of these typically change across holiday seasons and along with the yearly work calendar, while others grow and change along with the appearance of new trends and social circumstances that might not be related to your brand. One of the interesting details to note is that consumer groups have a different way of responding to social events, celebrations, and tragedies. While some prefer to keep their entertainment entertaining and don't like reality penetrating into their social media, others hold a grudge against businesses that fail to address the news around them. It's no secret that some brands go under fire for posting cheerful ads while news of tragedies strike the public. Some of your segments may stay neutral to this, others will appreciate a breath of fresh mood, and some might become enraged at your failure to react to the events around you.

You don't have to try and predict the directions to take with your advertising in these circumstances. Instead, you can search and analyze the audience's outlook on trends and social issues and base your reactions on findings that give the direct response to what you should do.

Facebook Targeting

The multitude of options for targeting the right audience ensures that you will get the best price for the right profile of your prospective consumers. The criteria that drive the most effective interactions with ads have proven to be location. With the history of web pages visited, as well as search engine history, the general demographic can be narrowed down to a granular demographic, which makes Facebook targeting ideal for both large and small businesses. This ensures full functionality and productivity of your investment in terms of budget, and it also improves your ability of resource allocation into the right segments of the audience as well as into the right aspects of the marketing campaign. This advanced targeting ability prevents you from delivering your advertisement to the wrong group of people.

Second degree targeting, or inferential targeting, allows you to determine the depth of your targeting strategy. This improves the personalization of your marketing and makes your campaign closer to the user.

Personalized marketing means that you are delivering to a very specific profile of a user, and the more your audience likes your advertisement, the more it will be shown. This only enhances the importance of creating a highly engaging and entertaining advertisement. The option for users to leave feedback on the advertisement gives you the opportunity to record the reception of your marketing campaign. Do your users like your ads? Do they find them interesting and enjoyable or do they prefer to remove them from their newsfeed entirely? This type of information is valuable for you to be able to further adjust your marketing strategy. This guarantees users an enjoyable experience and you the opportunity to take their feedback.

One of the aspects to look out for is the possibility of getting negative feedback. Facebook users are free to leave any type of feedback on the company's wall or page. If there's anything your consumer is unhappy with, no one can stop them from spreading the word to all your consumers within minutes. This also applies to advertisements, where users are quick to notice any inconsistency in the information given versus their previous experience with your company or product.

One of the strategies that companies use is to invite their fans to take their names or their friends' names and pictures of their products as a part of a competition in which they can win a reward. This is another strategy to expand your customer base which can be done either for free or through paid Facebook advertisements. While there aren't many negatives about this strategy, there are rules you should follow when creating what is called a competition or a giveaway.

Currently Facebook is testing the book bulk uploading tool which enables you to set up a multitude of advertisements without having to set up the parameters for each individual one. This will cut down the time it will take you to create an advertisement.

Social Media Personas

Social Media Personas

Do you want to know what your ideal customer looks like on social media? Defining your ideal audience is easier once you're aware of their typical social media features and behaviors. It will enable you to define your target audience with maximum specificity.

A *social media persona* is a face that represents a customer base, which allows you to better define your target customer base and market to them. It is relatively easy to create a social media persona. They are a fictional representation of your ideal customer base. This considers the demographics, pain points, desires, and an overall picture/image of the person to whom you're trying to sell. A social media persona represents a profile of your ideal customer.

Here's How Social Media Personas Can Help Your Advertising:

Boost Your Content Strategy

Social media personas can help you find your brand voice and publish relevant pieces, as well as to present that content in a way that will speak to your audience members. You can target different social media personas across different platforms, which is a segmentation strategy that allows you to connect to multiple customer bases. Segmentation allows you to connect with the different types of your audience in ways that are best suited for them. You can adjust the content style, esthetic, offers, advertising schedule, and everything else around the characteristics of different groups of your target audience.

How to Make Audience Data Campaigns Compelling

Organic reach is one of the greatest benefits of social media advertising. Granular audience data determines this success, if you use it properly to create compelling advertisements. Defining social media personas helps you collect the data needed to create such compelling content, which is the content that is tailored exactly according to the audience's needs, tastes, and preferences. To do this, you can use Facebook's granular targeting that is based on consumer age, location, interests, and other characteristics.

To Beat Fierce Competition, You'll Have to Tap into Niche Markets.

Now, how to identify your social media persona? The more specific you get with defining your ideal customer, the more success you'll have. Social media personas are based on the demographic specifics of your target audience. You can use this information as a starting point and then move to gather further relevant information that is less general and more personal. For example, what are their favorite colors? Which tone do they prefer? What are their typical needs and problems? An average student base will have a different profile than a customer base made of senior, retired people. Their slang is different, their sense of communication is different, and their taste in fashion and food is different. They value their money in different ways, with one valuing quality and others utility. You may rely on the millennial's fine taste and deeper pockets to invest in a quality, high-end product, but the retired group won't even consider the purchase unless they find it essential. In terms of content creation, you can use this information to create a line of ads that highlight the appeal and quality of the product for millennials and another set that highlights the long lasting and useful value of the product for the elderly.

So, How to Go About Defining Your Social Media Personas?
Do research and find out the attitudes, values, lifestyle, and spending habits of the group. You can go as specific as to break down their average look or daily schedule. Some groups are more uniform than others, but having any guideline is better than roaming in the dark. Some of the specifics include:

- fictional biographies

- personal features

- motivation

This approach enhances your chances of finding a format to cater to the audience that will satisfy the diversity of tastes. Social media personas help you adapt your brand messages and attract the most likely converting customers. In addition, this approach ensures the authenticity of your marketing. The last thing you want is to be accused of copying other people's marketing campaigns. Working from the unique knowledge of your audience and incorporating this information with your brand values is a perfect formula for originality. Here are the basic metrics:

Average age by group: How many customers do you have within each age group?

Geolocation: Where do they live? Are they scattered across different neighborhoods, or what can their location tell you more about their lifestyle and budget? What does geolocation tell you about tastes and preferences? If your audience is mainly urban, you can count on them to value efficiency, utility, variety, originality, while remote locations may suggest that your product or services are more appropriate for those who live at a smaller pace, valuing convenience, quality, durability, and lasting over visual appeal.

Are they dominantly male or female? Gender can tell you a lot about shopping habits and preferences, as well as visual taste and perception of utility. For example, men tend to feel more comfortable with experimenting when buying, while women tend to do more research and trust recommendations more than user manuals. You can leverage this information to decide whether you want to market your product as new and interesting or as proven to be effective.

Spending power. The spending power of your audience can be a great pointer to adjust your price and calculate any additional offers, discounts, and promotions.

Problems/pain points. One of your biggest goals with advertising is to learn how your product resolves a customer's problem and market that solution in the right way. In addition, the pain points can help you detect the obstacles the consumer might have to using your product.

Personality traits. Not only likes and dislikes but also features such as temper, attitudes, and values can help you frame your campaign properly.

Goals. One of the main goals for you to look for is what they're trying to achieve with money spending. There's a big difference in groups that spend to have fun and those that spend to gain value. Depending on your product, your advertisement should position your product or service in a way that aligns with the goals that are the most prevalent within the group.

Pet peeves/objections. What do your customers dislike about money spending and buying in general? Some of the more obvious objections are the lack of quality or a high price, while the lesser known include ineffective customer service, long waiting, or even lack of political correctness. Consumers are becoming increasingly sensitive to the issues of racial and gender diversity, as well as any aspects of the product, service, or the advertisement that fail to be inclusive. The more spending power the customer has, the more likely they are to pay attention to the aspects of the business beyond the appeal of the product itself. Don't be surprised to learn that your consumer base sees a great amount of relevance in how politically correct your business is in terms of diversity and inclusivity. On the other hand, they also might be sensitive to the way in which these messages are being worded and pictured. It's not uncommon for messages of 'higher meaning" to draw controversy if they're misworded.

Favorite brands. Looking into the other brands that your average consumer supports will give a great deal of information about the quality they're looking for and the aspects they admire in a brand. For example, skincare and makeup manufacturers are now paying more attention to environmental friendliness and racial diversity in advertising. If you detect that your consumer group supports brands that share the same values, it is a hint for you to showcase those values as a part of your brand.

Chapter 6: How to Design an Effective Facebook Ad

Choose Your Content Wisely

Every revenue-boosting social media strategy calls for outstanding content and effective content components. Facebook allows you to sponsor different types of posts and activities, depending on your business needs and purposes. The term "Ad' applies to many types of content, from sponsored posts, page advertisements, group promotions, to banner ads. You can even sponsor stories and group posts from not only your panel but other people's as well. Keep in mind that the content needs to be interesting and appealing to the audience it itself, meaning that promoting your brand products and activities won't be enough. You can choose across numerous ad types and strategies. Here are some statistics that point to consumer preferences when it comes to ad designs:

Some 30% of users prefer relevant information, while 18% like seeing relevant and captivating images. Nearly 17% of people surveyed liked videos. Text (pure information) and curated/edited content fall last with 18% of users preferring them. This points out the need to create authentic advertising content rather than using already available sources. The takeaway on preferred ad content is for you to showcase authenticity and employ the greatest levels of creativity when crafting written content, videos, and photographs that will be used for your ad campaign.

Create Effective Ad Content

Create Your Facebook Ad strategy

Brand exposure on Facebook is best done with a well-tuned advertising strategy. The hard truth when using Facebook to gain exposure is that you'll have to give it time. With an average click-through rate of 9%, you want to be careful about how you'll optimize our paid campaign. You need a perfect representation of your brand in order to effectively build and grow your business with ads.

Brand Awareness

With the greatest impact on the target demographic and the least interaction required, building up brand awareness is the best initial goal. Where to focus at the beginning?

You should focus on making your ad campaigns as cost effective and relevant as possible. With the budget, make sure to distribute your resources and determine the weekly and monthly spending limit. You want to avoid overspending on irrelevant clicks and traffic, which can happen if you don't tweak your targeting the best way.

Facebook ad relevance is the next topic to focus on. At first, you can target the broad audience to build brand awareness and then narrow down to the most relevant target group. The relevance of the ad can significantly impact this aspect of your campaign and remains crucial throughout the process. After researching the preferred demographic, you can proceed to narrow the optimization to the most effective members of the target audience. Throughout the process, it is important that your content offers something that is both familiar (addresses the existing situation or a problem) and the introduction of a new concept or idea. You should build your custom audience based on the measure that is the best fit for your content, and you should also tweak your content to meet the needs of the audience.

Get creative!

Following are the essential elements that make for a creative, authentic ad:

Identity. Your ad needs to be on brand in all its aspects. It needs to be effective in showcasing your business in terms of colors, logo, writing style and tone, as well as the way you choose to present your product or service.

Reward. What does the prospective customer gain from engaging with your ad and your brand? Ideally, your ad should promote something profitable for both you and the customer, such as a download (e-book, guide, whitepaper), a promo code, an offer, or a deal.

Tone. Make sure that the tone of your ad remains consistent across your platforms and that it aligns with your brand.

Call to action. Your ad needs to call for some type of action. Some of the actions include becoming a fan, signing up for your website, clicking the ad to visit the website, or shopping your product on the spot.

Serve your ads fresh

The ad needs to stand out in the customers' feeds, gaining attention among the post from their friends and family. Knowing that your target audience isn't specifically keep on clicking ads, do the best you can to keep the content updated. Make sure to have multiple concepts for the same ad, editing and tweaking periodically to freshen up the text and the visuals. This way, the viewer won't get bored with seeing the same advertisement each time they open their news feed.

Carousel ads

Facebook ads and pricing

Knowing how Facebook advertising prices work may intimidate you if you're not entirely familiar with the process and the functionality of the platform. Carousel ads are a specific format that allows you to combine multiple apps into a single unit. Facebook Carousel ads contribute to very favorable statistics when it comes to clicks and conversions. They have between 30% and 50% lower cost per conversion cost as well as 20% to 30% lower cost-per-click when compared to the single image ads.

It's their very nature which makes them eye catching, as they give you the opportunity to showcase a larger number of products. They are also interactive in nature, the same as other Facebook ad formats. The visual appeal of Carousel ads is obvious since having multiple ads shuffle in front of the eye of the observer is a lot more appealing than having only a single ad in front of their eyes for a prolonged period.

Carousel ads are efficient with any industry and any type of a marketing campaign. Still keep in mind that Facebook ad performance isn't equal across all industries and product categories. Specific industries also dictate cost for a click and the click-through rate of the Carousel ads. Although an individual or a business can run them, they aren't equally effective for everyone. For the effective use of Carousel ads, you should focus on the following:

Visual appeal. The imagery of your ads should be appealing to the eye and display brand identity. Loud colors and sleek appearances are recommended.

Variety of Products and Services Versus One

Carousel ads are generally a lot more efficient than the regular ones and you will spend less time setting them up. As an effective and a cheap option, they are a great choice if you are just starting out with Facebook advertising. However, an eye-catching element is crucial to make this as effective.

As with any other Facebook ad, you will start the process of creating the Carousel ad by defining the purpose and the goal of it. Next you will define your audience and do the usual targeting work. After that you will get to review your ad and make any desired changes, whether it's the images, the text, or any other aspect of the ad. There are a couple of important demands when it comes to a Carousel ad such as having to use square images that are 600 by 600 pixels. You can use up to 90 characters of text and you can use only 40 characters for your headline. Your ad description can contain only 20 characters.

Now is the time to set up your Carousel ads to perform well in terms of clicks, engagement, and conversions.

To secure the highest level of engagement, make sure that your photos all fit a single theme and are around the same concept in terms of warm shape and the visual effect. They should tell a story. Avoid using random pictures as you have no way of predicting how all these images displayed one after another will reflect in the eyes of the observer.

Pay attention to your color scheme. Wild colors will certainly draw more attention to your ad, but it is not always the best solution depending on the purpose of your ad, your product, and your industry.

As with other Facebook ads, the goals are equally important. Make sure to have a clear and well-planned goal in mind when setting up the Carousel ads.

Pay attention to your wording. Carousel ads don't leave much space for the app text so you will have to make sure that all the text you are using is highly impactful and effective. While you should avoid generic phrases and Calls to Action, you also must make sure that your content displays the brand's authenticity and fulfills all other requirements for effective ad copy. This means that the copy should also address some of the finer points of the customer and the benefits that they gain from clicking the ad and engaging with your business. This can be done using fewer words if you focus on motivating and uplifting phrases.

Don't make your ads too salesy. While sales may be one of your goals, it shouldn't be displayed explicitly in the ad.

How to Address Consumer Pain Points?

Your ability to identify and address the troubles and needs of your consumers is a good way to tailor your advertising campaign in a way that convinces the consumer that your product is the right solution.

The first step to address pain points is to help consumers identify that they have a problem. Next, you want to convince them that your brand has the right solution for that problem. While pain pointing is a simple process, your skill in crafting quality advertising is what will determine whether consumers will truly see your product as essential.

Effective marketing aims to solve problems related to pain pointing in multiple directions. Your consumer may have a wide range of problems that can be solved using your product, which means that you should focus on a couple of different types of pain points such as:

Financial. Issues regarding money are always big in the eyes of a consumer. You can address different types of monetary problems, such as not having enough funds for a needed product or service, or the need to reduce costs. Either way, your goal with addressing a financial pain point is to highlight the features of your product or service that are cost effective and help a consumer save money.

Productivity. Productivity is a big topic nowadays, and everyone is always after streamlining work processes and daily routines. Whatever your industry is, you can discover how your product enables the user to save time and do things faster.

Process. Improving the quality of work processes is also a big pain point for many consumers, be it crowdsourcing or running errands.

Support. Do your consumers lack support in certain areas of their life? Look into the features of your product or service that assists in urgent situations or with lack of knowledge and skill.

Identifying the audience's pain points will allow you to position your brand as a problem solver, signaling that you are essential for consumers to solve important problems.

How to Address Pain Points?

Your ability to address pain points in the right way is also important for effective advertising. The best way to do this is through good targeting and effective content creation.

To target your audience by pain points, investigate indicators such as inquiries in social groups and comments regarding solving the relevant problems, as well as searching for solutions to problems online.

To create the right ad for this type of audience, focus on highlighting the features of your product or service that address the pain point, and make sure to do it in a subtle, simple, and effective way. Pay attention to not come off as too salesy, generic, and self-serving. Remember that the ad should motivate the reader to visit your page or website, not conclude that you think of yourself as the leading expert on the subject.

Curate Content

Create a Community and Increase Engagement

The volume of content that is being published on Facebook is increasing drastically. As a result, the network is working to filter out the content in order to present the user with the most relevant and the most interesting pieces of information. Algorithm-wise, that means that "commercial" posts are now being filtered more rigorously, measuring the same parameters that you are using to target your audience. The good news is that both you and the network share the same goal in this sense: you want to reach the right amount of people for the purpose and you want the content to be relevant to the reader. For your part, you are trying to reach the audience that is most likely to respond. On the network's side, they are aiming for their users to have the most convenient experience. The downside of this is that now the chances of achieving organic reach are almost nonexistent. While you as a user might feel like numerous pages and commercial users are reaching you, think about the remaining hundreds of pages and posts you've "liked" since opening your account, looked once, and never came back. The main point of this is that you should, for the purpose of maximizing your efforts, start thinking of paid advertising as the only right way to stay continuously in touch with users. While your page might count tens of thousands, or even hundreds of thousands of likes, chances are that your nonpaid posts will only reach a couple of hundreds of users. That is, if you do a terrific job at designing them. Think about putting all resources into crafting fine content, researching and creating authentic visuals, dedicating the time to plan calls to action, only for all the effort to be in vain due to poor organic reach. You don't want this, do you? Neither do we. For the sake of maximizing the effects of your efforts, put a $ sign next to every single Facebook advertising idea.

Keep in mind to tailor all your advertising toward the customer and avoid self-promotion. Audiences aren't all that engaged with the brands themselves but more with whatever they gain from engaging with the brand. On the other hand, don't forget to keep yourself exclusive. Scarcity is recommended to keep the audience feeling like they are in some way special for engaging with you. Being personable to a degree is desirable, but a tender balance needs to be kept between staying personable and staying exclusive. You don't want to be overly personal and risk the audience viewing you as just another one of their Facebook contacts. While you should post ads frequently, as well as offer sorts of freebies, make sure to always have a level of exclusivity surrounding your brand.

The second thing to remember is to always remind the audience how to stay connected to your page. Be instructive and direct them to like and subscribe to you page. If you don't tell them, they most likely won't think of it themselves.

Now, let's talk about the increasing significance of video in terms of Facebook advertising. Facebook is an interactive platform, so it makes sense that the more interactive formats will attract more attention. Videos display multiple angles and sounds and give a better glimpse into the product or service. Whatever your industry may be, video ads in any shape or form (posts, stories, uploads, etc.) are most appealing to the users. Surely, it doesn't make any sense for a user to spend minutes looking at your ad picture. But, when it comes to video, users are more than happy to engage and share the content. Entertaining or visually mesmerizing videos captivate the most attention and engagement. Humor is the #1 factor of a compelling video, but visual beauty doesn't fall far behind either. Regardless how big the esthetic is in your industry, working to create a compelling video will show its fruits very soon.

Facebook Live

Facebook Live is yet another highly useful feature. People spend up to three times more time on Facebook Live ads than they do with the regular content. The sheer fact that the video is being transmitted *now* holds a lot of power in the eyes of a user. The element of scarcity raises conversion rates by 8%, while higher viewer interest and completion rates prove the point of increased engagement. Another benefit of Facebook Live is that the content is available only temporarily. Keeping in mind that the captivating content might soon disappear creates a sense of urgency which drives consumers to browse and shop more than they normally would.

Creating competitions is another way for you to increase engagement, as long as you abide by Facebook's strict rules and policies. Cross-promoting the contest between your social media profiles is also a good way for you to expand your audience.

Preferred Page Audience

Preferred page audience allows you to track your exact audience members and their interests, in order to reach them with better-tailored content.

Not being pushy is the most important thing when it comes to building engagement on your social media pages. While most small and medium businesses have social media accounts, not all of them are equally effective in seeing these accounts boost their company profits. Why is it so? The answer is in the quality and efficiency of their marketing strategies.

One of the biggest mistakes you can make when creating a marketing strategy is to base it on your needs versus the customer needs. Yes, your entire business is driven by your needs, but the way the product is presented to the viewer can make or break your advertising. While avoiding coming across as pushy, you need to tailor your social media strategy to your target and segmented audience. What does this mean?

First things first, you won't be able to use the same strategies across different social media platforms because the audience is different. Your Facebook audience might be completely different than your Instagram or LinkedIn audience, meaning that you must make a different strategy for each platform you're using. Second, the audience on a single platform isn't all the same either. While you might have a profile of a customer in mind, there might be subgroups within your broad group of audience members. If your audience captures members between the ages of 20 to 45, you are communicating with multiple different groups of people. You have young millennials, parents, entrepreneurs, stay-at-home parents, and many other subgroups. Here enters your task to trace the audience's; interests to be able to segment and decide how you'll tailor your marketing for each of the subgroups to appeal as much as possible.

Stats show that most effective posting includes one to posts per month. You should post more frequently only if you have over 10,000 followers. With more followers, frequent posts will reach different segments of the audience, finding a curious pair of eyes for any post. However, posting too frequently puts you at risk of being too pushy and repelling the audience members who might unfollow your page.

Rather than focusing on frequency, focus on the quality of your posts. While statistics that analyze the correlation between post frequency and engagement remain unclear, what is clear is that the quality posts drive significantly more engagement than poorly done posts.

Inspiration is another style you can use to drive engagement. Facebook users across different audience profiles appreciate inspiration content. The readers will identify with your posts, which is one of the most significant effects you're trying to create.

Your style needs to be consistent across different strategies and different platforms, as well as different audience segments. Stay updated with the mainstream events in your industry and also with the events that are relevant to your target audience. This way, you're creating a level of consistency that is essential for your audience to come back to your page. You are aiming to spark interesting and informative discussion, which will easily place your post, along with the entire comment thread, onto your users' news feeds, as well as their friends' news feeds. This is what makes the engagement element so essential. By sparking discussion, you are telling the Facebook algorithm that your post is relevant to the user. As such, it will quickly find its way onto surrounding news feeds.

The best times for you to post are one p.m. for shares and three p.m. for clicks, preferably on Thursdays and Fridays.

How to Use Page Insights

Using page insights, you can easily collect the data of those who are interacting with your page, including the exact numbers, age groups, and geolocation. Regardless of what the research says, page insights will give you a glimpse into the best times to post, since those times depend on the daily activity of your most active audience members. You will also be able to select the pieces of content that seem the most appropriate for your audience. Still, experimenting through trial and error will require openness to invest certain amounts of money without the prospect of seeing that money come back. For starters, you can choose to work with a smaller budget and smaller audience just to pinpoint the right samples to work with. Next, you can move to expanding the target audience and using more budget but with a clear image of what works and what doesn't work. If the prospect of experimenting with the advertising budget seems scary, think about how affordable Facebook is compared to other forms of advertising. In addition, the feedback and the possibility to analyze the effectiveness of your campaign also have a value on their own. This will prevent you from investing into ineffective campaigns in the future.

When it comes to calls to action, they require a bit more sensitivity and a more subtle approach. Audience doesn't appreciate aggressive, generic-looking calls to action. Much like the rest of your ad campaign, your call to action needs to address the benefit and the pain point. Shorter sentences and posts under 100 characters get up to 17% more engagement. This may be because of the audience's short attention span and the tendency to focus on shorter, easily digestible, simple-worded phrases rather than complex quotes and statements. Hence the fact that the extra short posts, composed of 40 characters, receive up to 86% more engagement.

A simple, yet effective technique you can use to do more with less in terms of the Facebook post is to write a vague statement that relates to the image or video that is linked to the post. Still, the statement should be in tone with your brand and strategy. While being vague, the statement should spark interest and emotion.

Make your posts skim friendly. Facebook users rarely visit the platform for quality, in-depth reads. Instead, they favor content that is easy to scan and understand in a split second. Regardless of the length of your post, make sure that it is well structured without blocks of text, and formatted so that your reader can get to the point without having to carefully read the entire post. If you're aiming to share a more complex, thorough message, having the key words and questions highlighted will ensure that all the readers "get the message", without having to go into reading the entire post.

This will make more sense after you learn that Facebook users tend to engage with the content without actually reading it. Regardless of the quality of your posts, a good chunk

f your audience might jump on the wagon, like, and share, even without reading the
post, if they identify something funny or important about.

Proactive Posts

The element of being proactive in Facebook posting means a couple of different things.
First things first, you are the one who has to initiate a discussion, as questions, and
spark interest. Other than that, your posts also need to be proactive in nature.
Actionable is one of the top-used words in association with digital content today. More
than making them think, Facebook users are leaning toward the type of content that
sparks a motivation to act. Hence the two most important elements of your ad: asking a
question and calling to action. In between those two, it is logical to place a piece of
informative content that explains the *whys* and the *hows* of the process. You can ask
questions in numerous ways, such as ones that lead to a blog post or relate to a
photo/video.

Become Personable & Accessible

Using personalized marketing, you are using audience analysis data in order to deliver
the most effective messages to your audience. This data includes interests and
demographics, as well as behaviors that prove to be most relevant.

Modern-day audiences prefer for the brands to view them as people, not as consumers.
If you manage to address customers as individuals rather than faceless consumers, it
could impact their purchasing decisions in a more positive way. How do you personalize
marketing?

Personalized marketing helps transform prospective customers into buyers. By
addressing the individual characteristics of a prospective buyer, you are reaching them
on a more personal level, creating a unique bond that is different than simply presenting
the audience with your product. Over half of your customers (74%) will be bothered if
you don't provide personalized web content, while over 60% of consumers worldwide
have a negative response to generic messages. Coming across as generic and money
hungry will surely impact your business in a negative way, according to statistics.

Personalized marketing helps you boost your relevance score and advertising costs,
simply due to the fact that the personalized messages instantly become more relevant to
your audience than the generic ones. This way, you'll receive more positive feedback to

your ads, automatically increasing the relevance score of your campaign and reducing the overall cost.

Personalized marketing also helps generating more conversions and leads, with a greater number of customers interacting with relevant, interesting ads and fewer passing your ad as annoying and irrelevant. Keep in mind that the network's primary goal is the satisfaction of their users, and that goal is way ahead of the profit they are making from allowing businesses to advertise on their platform. With this in mind, you can understand that the network will want to stimulate the businesses who are producing quality, relevant campaigns and delivering them to the right group of users by reducing the cost and charging more for those campaigns that are proving to be less relevant and less efficient, and that provide less quality to their target audience. Personalized marketing, as such, can help increase your social media ROI.

In addition, personalized marketing strengthens the brand affinity of your customers as well as their loyalty. When your consumers feel like you're recognizing their individuality, unique tastes, pains, and preferences, they're more likely to remain loyal and stay engaged with your brand in the long run. On the other hand, generic marketing campaigns that are targeting the wrong group of people risk the audience flagging the ads as annoying, uninteresting, or irrelevant, which increases your costs and reduces the overall success of your campaign.

Increasing brand awareness also becomes easier with personalized marketing. Once audience members identify your content as important and relevant, they'll be more likely to share the content and talk about it with their Facebook contacts, spreading the word about your business accordingly. Seeing a customer "tag" a friend in your comment section (keep in mind that you shouldn't ask the customer to do it) is a secure sign that you are winning the race, while receiving reports that the customers are removing your ads from their news feeds is a definite sign that you're doing something wrong with your campaign. Since more than 90% of consumers trust recommendations from close friends, mentions are the target goal. One of your strategies in this sense might be to craft a relevant, fun, informative ad that stimulates the reader to comment and tag a friend in the comment.

What Is the Takeaway Regarding Personalized Marketing?

Personalized marketing is all about learning the features of your target audience, segmenting in a way that addresses subtypes in order to create the most individualized content, which will automatically make it more effective.

How Do You Start with Personalization?

The best way to start personalizing your audience is to run data analysis of the audience. Next, you should create the buyer persona profile. To craft such a profile, pay attention to demographic data, likes and interests, activities on social media, the influencers that the audience is following, as well as their customer journey stage.

Keep in mind that simple demographic data won't be sufficient for a good audience analysis. The tactic of mapping out social media personas is crucial and delves into the interests, likes, and behaviors of the audience that speak about their personality and help you reach out to them more personally. Next, paying attention to the customer journey stage helps you separate those who are just getting to know your brand from those who have been following you for a long time. The first group will require less personalization and more informative content, while the latter will require a customized approach which relates to their previous customer experience.

Once you've done all this, move to collect all of your social media and online information about the audience to understand the typical characteristics and behaviors of your consumers. You can use this data to track the movements between your business page and your website. This way, you'll better understand the behavioral patterns of your customers, such as their purchasing choices.

Personalized Content

How Do You Create Content That Is Tailored Toward Your Social Media Personas?

You'll start with choosing the right format and the right topics. For this, analyze the engagement behaviors of your social media personas. Which media and posts are they most likely to interact with? Do they prefer images, videos, or text posts? Are they geared toward reading and commenting on articles?

Crafting Personalized Content

While the magic of personalized content might sound way too complex to grasp, you can start simple by brainstorming ideas and creating your own content library. Your content base should combine the interests of your customer base, as well as your brand messaging. After creating the formats of content that is geared toward your buyer personas, think about the best way to distribute this content. Now, we're talking about creating tailored posts. This is where A/B testing comes into play, which is a stage during which you'll measure the performance of your ads.

Measuring Customer Journey

You want to align your advertisements and their content with the typical stages of your customers' journeys, such as awareness, consideration, and conversion. Each of these stages will depend on the amount of familiarity your customer base has with your brand and whether or not they are ready to purchase. You'll use this information to create diverse, yet personalized ads that will be relevant to the different personas that make your audience. This is the type of audience that is searching for a product that will fit their needs.

Consideration Stage

The consideration stage is the stage of the customer journey during which they are considering whether or not to purchase from your brand, and your goal is to convince them that you are the right choice by offering the content that helps them address the pain points. At this stage, the consumer has most likely already interacted with your brand and posts. It is a good opportunity for you to collect data and run an audience analysis, which will help you with further creation of personalized content. You can also compare the current audience with the previously defined audience personas and use this information to publish problem-solving content. At the conversion stage, your goal is to convert those audience members that appear the readiest to buy. You can look into their on-site behaviors and see whether or not they've attempted purchase but given up for a certain reason. To appeal to the audience at this stage, you can use numerous tools on your website, such as coupons and individualized messages, such as pop-ups. It's also advisable that you use the followers' names and create personalized thank-you pages.

As a business, you're probably thinking in numbers, statistics, percentages, and strategies. But your customers make emotional decisions. Emotion is the most important aspect of shopping and identifying the sentiment of your audience remains crucial for a long-term relationship with consumers. Consumers want to feel like they are treated as human beings and like they matter. While they most certainly do, generic marketing can often present a brand as self-serving and turn consumers away. In the world of abundance of choices when it comes to brands to shop from, the consumers are paying more attention to brand values.

You can use social media to demonstrate your human nature and the values behind your brand in order to develop a long-lasting relationship with the consumer base. Here's how you'll become more personable on Facebook:

On-Brand Voice

The tone you are using to create advertisements shows even with the scarce 100-character Facebook posts. Tone is expressed through the general tone and emotion you're using, as well as the language, terminology, and hashtags. You should keep the tone consistent across your ads as well as your posts and comments.

Have Your Customer Service On Call

Responsive customer service is a major factor that determines the brand's image. If there's anything that customers complain about, it is the lack of responsiveness from customer service or the poor quality of customer service. Taking sufficient time to respond to consumers' questions and complaints will not go unnoticed. On the other hand, avoiding addressing issues, or worse, trying to censor consumer activities on your page to create a more favorable image, might backfire in controversy. Nowadays, consumers pay great attention to the online behaviors of brands, much like you're analyzing their behaviors. Rest assured that your loyal consumers, and also competition, keep track of your posting pace and mannerisms and they are very good at noticing any changes in patterns.

For this purpose, make sure that your page always has someone on hand who will act as a customer service representative and answer all customer questions. This might be challenging depending on the size of your page, and you don't have to answer all of the questions, particularly the repetitive ones. Still, you can assign someone to run your social media messages and respond to urgent messages, inquiries, and complaints, and for less urgent questions, you can block certain times on your calendar to answer the most popular questions. Your goal is to present yourself like a human who is contacting other humans, making the financial element less important when it comes to communication with your customers.

The Importance of Referral Marketing

Once your consumers trust you, they won't hesitate to recommend your business, which is the most effective way for you to grow and profit. Not only are the recommendations a free method to grow your business, but they are also the most convertible and the most effective.

Being helpful to someone on social media can create a positive ripple which travels far beyond that individual. In fact, you can look at this as a referral marketing tactic.

Be as transparent with your business as possible. Consumers appreciate transparency as it convinces them that you have their best interest at heart. One of the ways to showcase transparency with your social media and paid advertising is to showcase real pictures of your products, employees, and the overall work process. Consumers will appreciate a glimpse into your production, which is not only interesting and informative, but also convinces them that you aren't hiding anything from your consumers and that you're abiding by the rules of good practice. There are numerous ways to be transparent depending on your industry, but the best way to know what it is that you want to showcase is to address the customers' concerns regarding the industry. For example, if you're producing cosmetics, your audience may worry about the sanitation and the safety of your products. Here's a good opportunity for you to share the materials that show your quality control process. If you're working in the food industry, one of the major concerns could be hygiene and the quality of produce. Again, quality control and hygiene protocols can find a place in your marketing strategy to ensure your consumers that you have your sanitation and produce in check.

Learn Customer Needs & Preferences

By now, you have learned that an effective marketing strategy relies primarily on customer needs. You've also learned that you have to tailor your marketing toward the characteristics of your audience in order to bring your ads closer to them. Proceeding on this premise sets you up for a successful campaign that will be a win-win for both you and your customer.

What Do You Gain with Personalized Advertising?

At your end, what you are gaining from personalized advertising?

The effectiveness of the campaign.

With the abundance of time, effort, and resources that you'll invest in a quality Facebook advertising campaign, you want to maximize the chances of its effectiveness. While there's no way to guarantee that your advertising campaign will be effective, personalized marketing and meticulous targeting ensures placing the ad in front of pairs of eyes that are most likely to be interested in it and benefit from your offer. You as a business owner most likely distinguish window shoppers from those customers who are purchasing regularly and are actually contributing to the growth of your business. Metaphorically speaking, personalized advertising helps you draw more paying customers and fewer digital window shoppers. Even if your ad is top quality, if it's geared toward a wide audience that is less likely to engage, you'll see fewer lucrative results than if you pinpoint the exact group of users who actually need your business in order to improve their lives.

Better ROI and Allocation of Resources

With Facebook advertising, much like with other business investments, you can never be sure that your investments will pay off. The return on investment is never guaranteed, but strategizing with advertising helps you allocate resources and helps you balance out costs in a reasonable way, preventing you from overspending. After your data analysis, the glimpse into the results will tell you which elements of the campaign should be priority versus those where you can cut costs. For example, if your data analysis shows that your audience responds well to videos but has a high cart abandonment rate, how can you use this information to budget your campaign?

This information tells you that you should prioritize making quality video ads over posts and images. It also tells you that you should look into your website and make changes to make the access to your product easier, if the data suggests that consumers are facing a challenge or an obstacle, when visiting your website. From a budget point of view, these indicators direct you to the right amounts of investment that will be effective.

Permanent, Long-Lasting Engagement

If your goal is to build a loyal audience consumer base, which it should be, personalized marketing helps build a strong emotional bond and a sort of a partnership between you and the consumer. Once the consumer identifies that your business offers something beneficial, they will come back for more over and over again. Surely, this doesn't mean that they'll spend all of their money on your product, but it also means that you won't be easily replaced by the competition.

What Do Your Consumers Gain from Personalized Advertising?

Relevant Content They'll Enjoy Reading and Sharing

Consumers aren't too eager to use their platforms to promote others' businesses. They use social media to have a good time, and they'll engage with a business only when they feel like the business is a good representation of their own values and a trusted partner in overcoming problems and obstacles. You can become this partner to your prospective consumer whether you're selling office supplies, canned goods, or homemade cosmetic if you reach the exact people who need you constantly and on an urgent basis. To reach your target audience in this way, you'll need relevant content that is a good match to the reader's interest. When your reader identifies with your content, they will like, share and comment on the quality products and services they enjoy using.

One of the bigger moral dilemmas about targeted marketing is whether or not using people's personal information is justified. It is, if your intentions are honest and you're offering a quality product. In a broad sense of the word, your product is anything from a blog post to a service or a consumer good that is beneficial to the end user. When you put a good amount of effort into crafting quality products and quality content for you consumers, they will enjoy using your resources for a very long time. This way, you are profiting and doing a service to your consumers.

Facebook advertising is a good way to gear your product toward the audience base that is most likely to use it. But how to do that? There is a simple way for you to discover which base of customers will enjoy your product the most. You can target your campaign toward these users by using the following parameters.

Consumers who are already using your product. It's logical to assume that those who are already using your product are those who you should cater your advertising to If you're just starting to build your customer audience on Facebook, you can gear you ads toward those who have searched for your website or product online.

Consumers who are frequently searching for your product or a product in the same category. New to the market? One of the ways to expand your consumer base is to present the audience with your product but to go with the audience members who are already in high need of a product from the same category. Aim for those members who are engaging and posting frequently about your category of product, even if it's not your brand in particular.

Consumers who are fans of the product category in general. If your goal is to build brand awareness, and particularly if you're new to the market, aiming for sales and conversions might not be the most realistic and attainable goal. Instead, you can build up your follower base by targeting those audience members who have a general interest in your category of products. The smart way to reach these members is to not only go for Facebook likes but to also consider the audience behaviors and what they're posting about, targeting those audience members who are most likely to be interested in posting and sharing content related to your brand and industry. You can play detective a little bit here and look for signs of interests that go beyond likes and sharing. Look for behaviors such as researching the prices within your industry, but also pick up the information related to common problems and complaints.

Consumers who aren't familiar with the product but are researching a problem that your product can solve. Are you marketing a type of product/service that people don't think about before having an urgent need? If you're a dentist or a car repairman, it's most likely that your customers won't think of you before they need you urgently. One of the ways to reach this particular audience base is to look for those who are inquiring about the type of service you're offering and researching it online. Target words like "urgent" or "on call" to include this type of consumer into your marketing strategy. Ironically, a good portion of your prospective audience base doesn't have to be included in your campaign if you simply research likes and interests.

Chapter 7: How to Create a Facebook Ad Campaign Calendar

Time Your Posts Well

Organic content and reach remain a challenge when it comes to Facebook and the popularity and the saturation of the platform. Finding optimal posting times has been made more difficult with ever-changing Facebook algorithms. Luckily, there are numerous ways for you to detect the right time to post content. Some statistics show that the most engaging times, in general, are Tuesday through Saturday, between 8 a.m. and 3 p.m. However, this doesn't have to apply to your particular target customer base. The best way to calculate your ideal posting times is to look into the engagement pace of your current customer base. The rough stats suggest that you should focus your efforts on posting on Wednesdays between 11 a.m. and 1 p.m., as well as during the weekends between 9 a.m. and 3 p.m. Still, this brings up the question of whether or not your efforts will be effective when all of the other competitors follow the same advice? Will you stand out enough if you perpetually post during the same time as everyone else?

While looking into the activity of Facebook users does seem like a logical step, make sure to also look into other relevant statistics, such as:

- What are the times when the audience is most likely to interact?

- What are the times that the audience is most likely to shop?

- What are the times during which the users are most likely to make phone calls?

Make sure to follow your instincts and use common sense when timing your ads. For example, when you're posting an ad showcasing your services and asking for customers to call and schedule an appointment, does it make sense to time that ad during the weekends or evening hours or past your working hours? Can you count on your customers to save your phone number until the next day? With your budget on the table let's assume you can't. Hence, if you're posting and add advertising to your service, you should time it during your work hours or close to the target audience's work hours, so that they can make their appointment right away.

Based on this information, you can plan out your advertising schedule to increase the chances of successful interactions.

Budget Like the True Professional That You Are

This brings up the matter of budget. If simply pouring tens of thousands of dollars into your campaign would be sufficient to make it effective, advertising on social media would be extremely easy. Sadly, this is not the case. While dedicating a decent amount of resources into a campaign is desirable for optimal results, it is the allocation of those resources that plays a pivotal role. If you aren't careful, you can miss the mark by distributing your funds disproportionately to what's necessary and end up with a costly but ineffective campaign. So, how should you budget your Facebook campaign?

You can schedule publishing content both for a free or a paid option. You can schedule your posts straight from your page and choose the times based on the predicted customer engagement. Planning your post schedule helps you track and adjust engagement with your audience, noticing any flaws in the schedule.

Chapter 8: How to Track Ad Performance

Record Core Metrics

The data you collect is precious for countless reasons. Tracking customer response enables you to direct future ads properly in all aspects. Insights into your click-through rate tell you about the effectiveness of the ad and the appeal of the content, while the impressions help you notice how visible you are. Cost to Acquire lets you know about the overall spend of the campaign, which enables you to control the budget on a weekly and monthly basis.

Support Employee Advocacy

Encouraging employees to post about their work helps their friends feel more connected to the brand. Employees are more personable than a brand, which is a made-up construct. When your employees share information about your brand on social media, it helps the audience notice the face behind the brand. This helps you appear more relatable. You can formalize employee advocacy in different ways, but you can also encourage your employees to share company announcements and emails.

Track and Analyze Your Strategy

Keeping an eye on your metrics and determining the ROI is one of the next steps. Setting a realistic goal in terms of numbers and going back to see if that goal was met helps you establish whether or not your budget was well spent.

How to Plan Facebook Ads

ou need to plan your ads the same way you plan your entire work year, content, unches, and everything else. Planning ahead and having a strategy in place will help ou grow your business. Facebook ads are a great tool to support your launches and rowth. There are many ways for you to plan your Facebook advertising campaign.

our yearly plan can start by highlighting the most important monthly activities. Note l of your planned activities and figure out how you'll incorporate advertising into that chedule. The next thing you need to do is categorize your ads by types, determined by our business activities.

ext, use your research on the target customer engagement to plan and schedule dvertising dates and how you'll use the data for retargeting.

etargeting is a method of showing your ad to those who are already familiar with it and ave clicked on your site, or who have previously visited your page. Make sure to look at our calendar and organize the advertisements around your launches, prelaunches, ebinars, courses, etc. Make sure to note important observations from the campaign to eview your strategy for future campaigns.

 you're offering products or services that are always available, not just periodically, hich means that your goal is to build a list for that product, you can schedule regular ds for that product/service.

eep tabs on current trends and other advertisers' activities. If you feel like the major ompetitors, who are working with higher budgets, advertise at a certain time and could ffect your exposure, perhaps go for a time period that is not as saturated.

How to Use Facebook Analytics

The Importance of Retargeting

etargeting can help you increase conversions and reduce cart abandonment. The larketing strategy known as retargeting means going back with an updated version of our campaign to improve its efficiency.

 the attention span of your average customer decreases and the cart abandonment rate ncreases, this means more and more customers find it easy to give up on their shopping verall. The average abandonment rate is about 78%. This just shows how daunting it is convert visitors into shoppers. This also proves the importance of proper advertising ptimization after your initial efforts have proven ineffective.

What are the reasons for your visitors to give up on their shopping? This is the reason why remarketing is one of the best strategies to win your customers back. Retargeting enables you to notice and record some of the flaws in your initial campaign plan and to design a better one.

Facebook remarketing means running ads that are aimed at your past visitors. Using Facebook tracking pixel, you can identify the exact users that have abandoned your website. To increase the chances of your prospective conversions coming back, you can then use the offer of a discount or a promotional code. On a bright note, popular ad blockers that more and more users are installing on their computers aren't impacting the remarketing ads. However, remarketing doesn't mean that you should overwhelm your past visitors with aggressive ads as this might only turn them away. To begin with Facebook targeting, you will have to learn more about custom audiences and about using the Facebook pixel.

You can break down your remarketing to target very specific behaviors and user backgrounds. For example, you can use your current customer list and the previous visitors of your webpage or any other particular page. You can also target the users who used to visit your website but have stopped for a while. To do all this, you are going to have to create a custom audience. The purpose of creating a custom audience is to profile the people who are already interacting with your business and a website.

If you already have a list of prospects, you can upload it to your ad manager using the option to select the customer file. You can also use your own customer data file.

Here's How to Prepare Your Customer Data

You'll start by focusing on your website traffic and utilizing your Facebook pixel. The Facebook pixel is that tracking code which you can use to record the behaviors of Facebook users on your website. You will have to copy and paste the code onto your website. To use this feature, you will have to become skillful in using Google Analytics. To use the retargeting pixel on Facebook, you will have to select the website traffic which will allow you to segment your audience. You can both include and exclude certain URLs and other behaviors you find irrelevant. After creating your custom audience, you can adjust the site and other platforms or simply integrate the pixel.

Facebook provide enough instructions for you to successfully install the pixel but here are some useful guidelines anyways.

You can choose specific codes for specific actions—for example adding a cart on your website. After the pixel becomes active, you will be able to trace the activities on your ad manager. With the multitude of variables, your work with the process isn't going to be fast, but it isn't complicated either. This way your customer will feel like it has been tailored specifically for them.

he amount of attention that you devote to your custom audiences can do a great deal or the efficiency of the retargeting process. Importing your email list is the initial step ou can take to ensure that all of your current customers are included in your dvertising campaigns and that those who are engaging lightly with your business are gularly reminded that you are still there for them. Finally, remarketing gives you the est insight into your top-performing ads and campaigns. Those are the ones that you nouldn't change and should replicate to secure maximum success.

acebook offers you a full set of analytic information that you can use to check the fficiency of your campaign and website. This information includes the identities of your ebsite visitors as well as the behaviors on your page and your website. Facebook Ads lanager is a feature that will allow you to review your advertisements and analyze their erformance.

stablishing Objectives with Facebook Ads

you choose the brand awareness type of ads, you will let people know about your offer, s well as the unique features of your brand and business. This is a good option for eginners.

you choose a reach option, the algorithm will work to deliver your message to the reatest amount of people possible. If you already have built brand awareness, the reach ill give you a great level of coverage.

ow to Create an Ads Set with Facebook Ads Manager

lere are some short instructions for creating your ads set:

ame your ad set

he act of naming your ad set is simple, but if you choose to work with multiple ad sets, s you should, then naming your ad set after relevant targeting details isn't a bad idea.

argeting

his is the part where you'll apply all the knowledge about targeting the right audience. he Ads Manager will allow you to choose the audience members by multiple categories, ıch as a location, age range, language, gender, and interests by keywords.

Since the aim is to target the audience that is the most likely to benefit from your ad, you want to avoid coming across as generic. Meaning, go for the audience that will show interest in your content rather than those who'll find it irrelevant.

Target by detailed features relevant to a group

Facebook Ads Manager will allow you to identify and target the exact groups of users who are the most appropriate for your market.

Choose the connections to follow

Other than behaviors related to your page, you can identify the best audience members by including the behaviors they express elsewhere online. Using the search bar in your targeting window, type in the names of pages, people, and events that the users are following.

Determine whether or not you want to include your current followers into the campaign, and check off or not the followers of your page and the members of your groups

Ad placement

Now is the time to choose where your ads will be placed. Here's how you'll choose where to place your ads:

Go to the placement section of the Ads Manager and choose the right options. Be careful in analyzing the options that are being offered and make sure to review the ad in order to check which placement suits it best. You can choose to place your ads onto news feed, instant articles, or suggested videos. The system of the Ads Manager will help you make this decision.

Price your ad

While you shouldn't overspend on your ads, giving them a decent value will help you increase the chance of your ad showing up on the user's pages.

Choose whether or not to place ads on Instagram

With Facebook now being linked to Instagram, the Ads Manager will give you the option to include Instagram ads in your campaign as well. Think carefully about this option and whether or not it actually fits your goals and overall campaign.

Choose devices

When creating your marketing plan, you've most likely defined which devices you want to cover with your ads. Keeping in mind that different devices have different conversion rates and overall metrics, choose whether or not you want your ads to be shown on desktop, mobile, or tablet, or you want to cover all devices available. Keeping in mind that the Facebook users are using the network primarily for their mobile devices these days, it would be wise to focus your ads on mobile and tablet users.

Allow or disallow Facebook to choose ad placement

The idea behind the Facebook algorithm is to choose the best placement for your ad. However, the algorithm can behave in unpredictable ways, which is why you should decide whether or not you'll allow Facebook to determine the ad placement or you'll do that yourself.

Use the power editor

You can use Facebook's feature known as the power editor to review the entire campaign in one place. You can also use it to create new ads. To do this, open the editor and click the ads section. Now, click to create a new ad, and choose whether you'll start a new campaign, or you will edit the campaign that is already set up.

Fill out the information boxes with the preferred ad features. Now, you can adjust the physical layout of the ad like the photo size, the amount of text that will appear, as well as the additional buttons that will be displayed. After you've finished editing your ad, review the ad.

Here are a couple of useful options that the ad manager will give you regarding the ad design and content:

Convert existing content. You can use the content that already exists on your page to create an ad. You can choose to boost an existing post and review it to see how it looks as an ad. To do this, go to your Ads Manager dashboard and choose the Use Existing Post feature. You will be forwarded to your page, where you will review your posts and decide which ones you want to use as an ad.

Add offer ads. Offer ads are a type of ad that shows people that you are offering something to your customers. This type of an ad will show a button that links to your website and a description of your offer (discounts, promo code, etc.). To create an offer ad, select the options traffic, conversions, and store visits as the ad objectives. Next, click the offer button. Select the page that you will place your ad on. Insert the specifics of your offer and click create to see a preview of the ad. Next, you will enter all other targeting and placement information and determine the schedule when the offer will be posted online.

After you've finished creating your ad sets, click the place order button and you've officially created your advertising campaign.

Offer a Promo Code

What if there is a promo code that you want to offer to your users? To insert a promo code into your ad, click the create offer option and offer redemption, and use the unique codes option to upload the CSV button, which will enable you to enter the file containing the promo codes. After you've done that, click the create button and your promo code is set!

Budgeting for Your Ad Campaign

How to think about the budgeting of your Facebook ad campaign? On the one hand, the will to invest is admirable. On the other hand, the idea of failed investment is a risk to protect yourself from. So, how do you stay open to investment but effective in allocating your resources with your campaign?

First things first, your budget needs to align with the revenue of your campaign. If you're just entering the market, aiming to profit substantially may be less probable, but your goal should be to at least break even. Thinking within these terms, start with reviewing your current position in the market and your consumer base. Are you a start-up? If so, your idea of revenue should align with building brand awareness, engagement, and building up your portfolio/reviews. If you're an established business, you can consider more lucrative amounts when weighing in investment and profits. Luckily for you, Facebook is also aware that the user's success is their success. Meaning, they are on your side and willing to show you how to budget your campaign. Facebook is introducing a new feature to help advertisers track their budget, called the Campaign Budget Optimization. Simultaneously, Facebook is starting to reduce the costs of successful ads in order to reward quality ad creation and thoughtful targeting. It is their way of rewarding the advertisers who are trying hard to deliver value to their readers. While the Facebook algorithm might be going against your interest, there are numerous features of the Ad Manager that work for you in terms of helping you to design and deliver your ads, such as tracking pixel, budget optimization, and a vast amount of targeting options. To budget your campaign successfully, make sure to use these features to the greatest extent. After all, they are there to make your job easier.

Campaign Budget Optimization

acebook created the CBO feature to help campaign creators run profitable campaigns. ou can use different strategies to increase your profitability. The best uses for ampaigns is to control costs on a campaign level instead on the ad set level.

he best CBO campaigns have the following advantages:

- broad range
- broad cold interests
- super lookalikes
- Facebook will decide which ads to prioritize
- broad range
- good for testing lower budgets and tests which will prove a priority

ou will select an ad and create a CBO that includes all relevant geolocations and nguages, creating multiple ad sets by age groups. Scale and test your campaign by age roups and go back after a couple of days to check the optimization for most relevant ds. Next, you want to create a new CBO campaign that includes the most relevant terest-based ads on the Facebook Audience Insights. Next, you want to create dditional ad sets according to your plan. Based on insights, you can then calculate the stimated costs of the entire campaign. The main point here is to replicate the profitable ds and eliminate less or nonprofitable ads.

Iow Much Money Should You Spend on Facebook Ads?

t the very least, your Facebook campaign will be profitable when the revenue you gain om it exceeds the money you have invested. While your ROI goals should be realistic, ou should have a profit in mind when designing your campaign. While some profits are leasurable, like an increase in sales and leads, others like brand engagement and brand wareness are less measurable but potentially more profitable. With this in mind, rather lan setting your budget in stone and aiming for accurate numbers to come back, you hould aim to set up your campaign budget to allocate the funds to the most effective dvertisements and to eliminate the noneffective ones. So, how do you start with udgeting your Facebook campaign?

)efine the Revenue

Regardless of the size of your business, calculating the potential revenue is the initial step that you can take instead of setting a sum of money aside and testing the results. With a revenue goal in mind, you'll be able to track not only the effectiveness of the campaign in general but also the other relevant factors that are driving more or less spending. Strategizing, tracking, and optimization are crucial to designing profitable Facebook advertising campaigns. Particularly, because the engagement itself isn't a relevant indicator of profitability, but rather an indicator of potential for profitability. Keep in mind that social media activity related to your ads doesn't have a direct connection to revenue. Ultimately, what you'll define as revenue depends on the aspects of your business that are measurable, such as sales, subscriptions, appointments, etc.

You first need to answer the question of how much budget do you need in order to generate a particular figure of revenue with Facebook ads. This way, you'll calculate your ROI more accurately. For example, for a $1000 of revenue on a $10 margin of your product, you will need a 100 sales/month. Next, you want to set a monthly revenue target for your marketing campaign. If you know that you need 12 leads on average in order to make one sale, you will aim for 1200 leads, meaning that each lead will cost you $0.80. With the revenue goal now set, you can move to configure the Facebook Ad Manager according to the necessary data. The Facebook pixel will allow you to track conversion and provide the accurate ROI. After you've set up the pixel, you can move to create a custom conversion. You will create a customer conversion by choosing the option in your measure and report column. To track the conversions, enter the URL of the thank-you page into the pop-up window and select the "Lead" category. Name your conversion, and any recorded leads will now be available for you to review.

To create customer conversions, you'll choose Conversion as the campaign objective and for the conversion event, you'll choose custom conversions. Now, your ad spend is set up to generate leads.

A Two-part Campaign

When calculating the CPL (cost-per-lead), everything from your audience to ad quality and the funnel strategy will affect the outcome. You should carefully choose whether to send the cold audience directly to your sales page or use a lead magnet and retarget your readers.

Monitor and Adjust

After running the ads and gathering the conversion data, you can look at the cost of your Ad Manager. Configure the columns for custom conversions to track the relevant data.

To use the customized columns, select all the relevant check boxes that you want to add to your results. Make sure to save your settings and then apply them. The results will show you your cost per lead. Now, it's time to revisit your revenue goal and review your ad budget.

After reviewing your budget, proceed to refine your ad campaign to better fit your goals and improve your results. Choose your best performing ads and amplify the amount you'll display considering your goals and budget. Some users prefer to increase slowly by reviewing every couple of days, while others, mainly those who are more experienced and work on a more comfortable budget, amplify their successful ads to five or more times. Look into the metrics and see which keywords brought you the most success, eliminating those that were less effective. Keep in mind that displaying the ads, even without any engagement, also affects the budget, so you want to eliminate all of the parameters except for the most successful ones. Based on your results, create lookalike audiences that expand in numbers but contain the same characteristics as those leads who've filled out your forms. Create separate lookalikes for those leads on different consumer journey stages. Meaning, you want one lookalike for those who've only clicked on the ad, a separate one for those who've filled out your form, and one for those who've already made the purchase. Your goal is to expand the audience and deliver the ads to those who are the most similar to your successful target audience.

You'll do this again in your Ad Manager by clicking "Create Audience" and choosing the "Lookalike audience" option.

What About Your Conversions?

If you're a beginner, and you had any conversions for starters, congrats! It is not an easy job. Conversions show you that you've hit the mark with at least a portion of your audience. But what to do next? You want to draw insights from this base, record their main features, and again replicate your advertising pattern to expand it to a greater number of viewers.

What Is the Takeaway?

While it is true that you can't be scarce when it comes to funding your Facebook campaign, being overly relaxed about it isn't wise either. Not only does poor targeting result in an ineffective campaign, it also takes away the ability for you to learn precious information about the convertible audience. Lookalike audience, social media persona, segmented audience, all of these terms have a slightly different meaning but boil down to the same pattern: tracking the effective parameters using a smaller budget and then magnifying the budget to include the greater number of audience members who are most likely to convert. So, what is the pattern that we recommend?

- Define a realistic revenue for your long-term and short-term goals.

- Calculate the lead cost based on your findings.

- Apply all of the research and knowledge when targeting the audience, starting from a smaller budget.

- Pick up the results after a couple of days and analyze the ads.

- Choose the most effective ads and settings and replicate, only to an increased audience.

- Rinse and repeat until you meet your goal.

- Go back and analyze the entire cost of the campaign, drawing the conclusions that are relevant to your industry and business.

Chapter 9: Facebook Ad Strategies

Now that you have learned all the details about creating effective Facebook ads, it's time to learn about various strategies.

Pay-Per-Click Strategy

The Pay-Per-Click (PPC) strategy is one of the most commonly used strategies which allows a company to pay only when their ad is clicked. This strategy helps businesses in several ways. First, you know your money is put to good use. A lot of people are cautious about putting money toward advertising because they don't know how useful it will be. This is often more important to people who are just starting their company. Because their advertising budget is often low, they don't have money to put toward highly effective ads. This strategy allows them to do this without having to worry about wasting money on an ad no one is looking at.

Second, you are able to keep great analytics from pay-per-click advertisements. This factor will only help you create a stronger target audience. You can learn more about the location of your audience, their age, gender, and interests. Then, you will take this information and improve your advertising to focus more on your target audience. You just want to be careful to not put too much emphasis on just your target audience. You always want to find a balance of keeping your target audience engaged and pulling other people into your ads and business. This is one of the best ways to help your business grow.

If you are interested in trying the PPC strategy, Facebook easily lays the steps out for you in the Facebook Ad Manager.

1. You want to select your objective. You will need to look at where you are with your target audience and your goals. After you have a thorough understanding of what you want to gain from your PPC ad, you can look at the marketing objective offered by Facebook. There are three main objectives which are based on where the buyer stands at that moment. The awareness stage objective focuses on bringing awareness to your brand and outreach. The consideration stage objective focuses on increasing traffic and installing apps. The decision stage objective focuses on product sales and store visits.

2. You will select your audience. In this step, you will customize your audience with the options Facebook provides. Your first option is basic targeting, which focuses on gender, age, and language. Your second option is detailed targeting, which focuses on interests, demographics, and behaviors. Your third option is connecting to your targets. This means you can connect to people who like your page, their friends, and people who have visited your Facebook business page.

3. After setting your target audience, you will look at ad placement. Where you choose will depend on your company. For instance, if you are starting out, you will want to a more general ad placement as this will allow you to collect data and get an idea of the best places for your ads.

4. Before you give your okay to place an ad, you will need to set your schedule and budget. This option is completely up to you. You can choose how much money to spend per day and how long the ad will run. For example, if you decide to spend $5 per day and run it for 10 days, you will spend about $50.

Advantages of the PPC Strategy

Facebook's global audience is one advantage to the PPC strategy. There are over 2 billion people which use Facebook's platform every day. Most of these people spend close to an hour of their day on Facebook, which increases their chances of seeing your ad.

Another advantage is your target audience. Through the PPC strategy, you will be able to create your target audience, which will allow you to become more detailed with your ads later. You can decide how you want to focus on your target, such as age, behaviors, location, or interests.

PPC strategy gives you a lot of detailed analytics, which you can use to determine your ad's effectiveness. Some of the analytics supplied are clicks, reach, and impressions.

Disadvantages of PPC Strategy

One disadvantage is the PPC strategy is not free, which can make it tough for small businesses or nonprofits to use. Many businesses will do anything they can to stretch their pennies, so they won't take part in a lot of paid advertising.

A second disadvantage is PPC cannot guarantee that people will visit or purchase products from your business. It can help get the word out about your store, but unless you are able to pull customers into your store with your ad, there is no guarantee of an increase in sales.

Finally, you can lose a lot of money through Facebook's PPC strategy if you are not careful on how you create an ad. If you want to create a great ad with PPC, but you are not creative enough or don't understand the basics of advertising, you might need to pay someone to create the ad.

Facebook Messenger Ads

Facebook Messenger holds a lot of great advantages, such as connecting to your customers instantly, and helpful features. Facebook Messenger Ads is a bit different from other types of advertising options on Facebook. Instead of forcing your audience to click a link to get to your Facebook page or website, they can start an instant conversation with you. There is no need to worry about being unavailable to answer right away because you can also set up automatic responses to certain questions. Of course, you won't be able to set up responses for every question, but this doesn't mean it's not an engaging feature. In the course of a month, there are about 2 billion messages sent from customers to businesses using Facebook Messenger ad ("16 of Our Most Powerful Strategies For Advertising On Facebook", 2017).

There are two types of Facebook Messenger Ads.

1. **Click to Messenger ad**. This is a typical type of ad that will show up in a user's messenger. In order to connect with your business, they will click a link which will open a messenger chat box.

2. **Sponsored Messages.** This type of ad shows up in a user's messenger chat box. It is the most common type of Facebook Messenger Ads as a user doesn't have to take much action to get a reminder about sales or ask a question.

Creating a Facebook Messenger Ad

Facebook's Ad Manager runs its Messenger Ads, which helps make the process of creating an ad easier. In order to create a Messenger Ad, there are eight basic steps you need to perform.

1. Once you are logged into your Facebook Ads Manager, click the "+" tab.

2. Select your marketing objectives. There are three categories for your goals, which are awareness, consideration, and conversion. Under these categories you will want to select the goals for your ad. For example, you can select awareness, reach, engagement, messages, traffic, and catalog sales. If you aren't sure what you want to focus on, take time to look into each one of these and think how they will help you build your business.

3. Select your type of messenger ad. This is where you will select information such as choosing whether you want your ad to be a sponsored or click to messenger ad.

4. You will describe your target audience. Before you get to this section, you need to ensure you have created your ideal customer. In this step, you will choose gender, age range, location, and behavior. You can create a target audience which is specific or general. It is important that you make sure you include everything you can about your target audience. Facebook will use this information to help select people to show your ad to.

5. From your ad type, Facebook will prepopulate choices for your ad placements. In this step, you will pick where you want to place your ad, such as messenger, stories, or inbox.

6. You will then set a schedule and a budget. You will pick the amount you want to pay per impression throughout the whole ad or daily. You can run your ad as long as you want. Keep in mind, that you can choose to extend an ad as well. For instance, if you are not sure how well your ad will perform, but find it performs well, you can add on a few more days. You can also pause an ad if it's not performing well.

7. Next, you will design your ad in any way you want. For example, you can use text and an image or just text. When using text, you will want to make sure you keep your target audience in mind and use words that will pull them into your ad. Ensure that your image is eye catching and connects with your business or product.

8. Now, it is time to launch your ad. You can set a day for your ad to start or post it immediately. Make sure you take the time to analyze the statistics of your ad. Notice the engagements you are receiving, including when people are most likely to view your ad.

Advantages of the Facebook Messenger Ad

One advantage is the sales opportunities for your ad. Because you can advertise in messenger, your ad is unique. This can easily pull in more customers because they take notice of the new type of advertising.

Another advantage is you can increase personal communication. People don't have to post on the wall your business's Facebook page when they have a question or concern. Instead, they can receive instant communication with your automated messages or you through a private message.

Disadvantages of the Facebook Messenger Ad

One disadvantage is that people feel like the ads are too big. They don't appreciate going to their messenger and only seeing an ad from a company. Because of this, they could elect to hide the ad.

Another disadvantage is that a lot of people feel the ads are irrelevant to their interests, which can happen for various reasons. For example, you might not be able to select the right target audience for the ad or Facebook's algorithms are not performing well for this ad's experience.

Evergreen Facebook Ads

Evergreen Facebook Ads help you repurpose a previous ad. Many people feel they constantly need to create new ads for Facebook. This can become a challenge for most businesses, especially when you change your ads weekly. If you have a previous ad that you like but want to change it up a bit, then you should try Facebook's evergreen ad option.

Three Evergreen Ad Strategies

The purpose of changing a previous ad is to make it more engaging. This can be challenging for many people. Fortunately, Facebook's team is always doing what they can to make your experience easy and enjoyable. In order to make the best out of your evergreen experience, you will want to focus on one of these three strategies.

1. **Lead Generation Campaign.** If you have an established business with ads that are highly engaged, you will look at the lead generation campaign. You use this strategy when you want to expand your customer contact list. You will pull your audience in by requesting their email address so you can give them a free online catalog or sign up for a webinar.

2. **Awareness Campaigns**. You will use awareness campaigns when you are trying to get people to notice your business. You will want to use your brand's story in order to pull people in and get them to engage in your advertising and Facebook page. You can use this strategy continuously. As you continuously run an awareness campaign ad, you will increase your customer database and your sales.

3. **Conversion campaigns**. In this strategy, you will try to close a sale with people who engaged in your ad. In order to make yourself stand out from your competition, you will want some type of great sale on a few products or offer a first-time buyer bonus. For example, you can allow all first-time shoppers to take 30% off their whole order.

You can run more than one evergreen ad. For instance, you can always have an awareness campaign ad going and then switch between the other two strategies.

Creating an Evergreen Ad

There are a few certain steps you will want to follow when you are creating an evergreen ad.

1. You will want to establish your campaign goal and trigger. For example, you might run an advertisement where people can sign up for a free webinar.

2. You will customize your target audience. You can focus on any demographics, but you should ensure that you are creating the right target for your repurposed ad. When you are in this section, you will select the trigger. For instance, what can they register for or what product can they purchase for engaging in your ad?

3. Now, you will select more details for your goals. You will choose what you want to focus on with this ad, whether it is engagement, reach, or conversion.

4. You will then set your schedule and budget. You can allow Facebook to send the ad automatically to a user's wall if they fit within your target audience or you can select the number of impressions you want daily.

5. You will then decide where you want to place your evergreen ad. For example, you can place an ad on a user's Facebook feed, their Instagram account, or their instant articles.

6. You will then make the ad go live. As the advertisement runs, you will be able to analyze your statistics.

dvantages of Evergreen Ads

he first advantage is you don't have to recreate a whole new ad every time. You can find previous ad which did well and recreate it with the same idea or image.

nother advantage is you are able to see how well your evergreen ad is performing ompared to the first time you launched the ad. This can give you insight on if your dvertising creativity is growing and which ad pulled your target audience in more.

isadvantages of Evergreen Ads

ne disadvantage is that you can become too dependent on recreating old ads. While iis strategy is useful, you don't want to stop creating whole new ads.

nother disadvantage is that you can become dependent on creating new ads from old ds. While Evergreen is a useful technique, you want to ensure you are keeping up with ie current trends in advertising. When you take from old ads, you can focus more on ie old trends than newer trends.

ocus on Different Platforms

acebook uses various platforms because their users log onto Facebook through ifferent devices, such as a desktop, phone, or iPad. Even though most people use the iobile app for their Facebook experience, desktop users are still common. If you only ay attention to one platform, you could miss a large part of your target audience. This asically means you want to ensure your ads are optimized for both desktop and mobile istomers.

Vhen it comes to Facebook, there are various levels of customer awareness, which are onnected to the platforms.

1. **Unawareness** is the first level which includes people who are completely unaware of your company and product or haven't established a reason to look into your product. For instance, in order for people to care about your product they need to see a need or want for it. If they don't need your product to solve problem, they aren't interested.

2. **Problem aware** is the second level and focuses on people who know they have problem. However, they are unsure where to look for a solution.

3. **Solution aware** is the third level and includes people who found a solution, but not because of your company or product.

4. **Product aware** is when users have identified how your product can help them solve their problem.

5. **Most aware** is when users have purchased your product and become your customer. They now believe that the best way to solve their problem is through your product.

When it comes to these five levels, there are certain devices which are more appropriate for some levels. For example, people are more likely to be in the levels of product and most aware when they are on a desktop. When they are using a mobile device, they tend to be on the level of solution aware.

Combine Content Marketing and Facebook Ads

Most business owners want to jump into the Facebook advertising phase as quickly as possible. When this happens, they run the risk of establishing the wrong target audience and creating an unexpressive ad. This can lead Facebook to place your ad on the wrong user pages. This will lead to low engagement and you struggling to build up your customer base.

One strategy to use that will help you skip the beginning struggles of Facebook advertising is to combine content marketing and Facebook ads slowly. For instance, you will start by sharing valuable information about your company to your target audience. When you do this, you don't need to try to pull them in with a sale or free product. You don't even need to try to get them to sign up for anything. Instead, just put your business out there. Focus on your mission. For instance, if you are a nonprofit which reaches out to rural communities in your area with various services, like free counseling and a food pantry, you will want to include this.

he amount of information you will share in the ad is limited, so you need to ensure you re writing catchy content. You want to include words that will make people stop crolling and take note of the advertisement. For example, if you are a food pantry, place his in your content. These are two words that quickly capture a person's attention. eople either need to use food pantries or they like to donate food.

ou will want to make sure you have eye-catching images on your ad as this is typically hat makes people stop scrolling. While you might feel your building is the best choice, people don't know your business exists, they might not pay attention to a photograph f a building. Instead, you want to use an image that connects to your mission. For xample, you can use an image of food or inside of a food pantry to catch a person's ttention. People need food to survive, so they are guaranteed to pay more attention to n image of food than a building.

ou will also want to have a link which will take them to your website or Facebook page. lere, you will want to have more information directly at the top of the page. You want to take sure everything is easy to find as people won't spend a lot of time looking at your te. It will help if you strategically place information and pictures on your website in rder to keep their attention.

's also important to do more than just launch your advertisement. A lot of people feel nce they hit the "post" button, everyone is going to see it. This isn't true. In fact, the lore you get people to share your ad, the more engagement you will receive. Request our friends and coworkers to share the advertisement on their Facebook page. You ould also request potential customers to share the information while they are scrolling arough your page. If you do this on your website, you want to have a Facebook button eadily available or a way they can share the ad quickly. People are more likely to share aformation if all they have to do is click a button or two.

Chapter 10: Keeping Your Customers Engaged

Your Facebook advertising is going well. You have doubled the size of your customer base within the first three months of opening a Facebook page for your business. You are starting to learn what ads are more interesting for your customers and you know your top strategy. While it is easy to find yourself basking in your new glow, you don't want to start relaxing yet. In fact, you still have a lot of hard work to accomplish if you want to run a successful business.

Once you pull customers in, you need to hold their attention. To do this, you need to become creative in keeping your current customers engaged. Even if they rave about your product or service, this doesn't mean they won't leave for a different company. Customers need to feel that they are the most important part of your business. If they don't, they will leave. In order to make them feel this way, you need to continue to put effort into showing them you enjoy having them as a customer.

Strategies to Keep Your Customers Coming Back

1. **Social media** is one of the first strategies you can use to keep your customers engaged. The great advantage is this is already at your fingertips through your Facebook account. Other than placing more ads, you want to remain in contact with them. Social media is a great way to do this as it allows you to communicate with your customers immediately. Whether you are on Facebook and use messenger or Twitter, your customers can message you when they see your post. You can then receive a notification of their comment or message and respond back immediately. This psychologically tells customers that they are extremely important to you. This will make them feel good, which will improve their feelings about your product and company.

2. **Stay in contact.** It is easy to continue to post on your Facebook page or run ad every week. However, if you don't actually stay in contact with your customers, they are going to lose interest in your company. Staying in contact means that you converse with your customers one-on-one or in a group. This can mean you reply to their comments on your Facebook page along with their messages. Don' lose sight of ensuring you focus on your customers individually.

3. **Surprise your customers** by going above and beyond what they initially expect from you. Customers believe that you are going to forget about them. Take

this opportunity to prove to them that you won't. You can do this by sending them coupons for products or a thank-you note or remembering their names. Of course, with all of your customers it will be hard to remember everyone's name. However, you might be able to put a name and face together with your top customers. Another way to surprise your customers is to send them a birthday wish or simply do something a little special for them. When people are surprised, they get excited and are more likely to recommend your product or service.

4. **Make customer service your top priority.** When customers believe they are number one in your book, they are more likely to return if they know you can help them. In order to maintain the best customer service possible, you want to strive to make 100% of your customers happy. Of course, this is a lot easier to say than do. One of the best ways to do this is to always be polite and respectful. Even if you receive a negative message or comment from an unhappy customer, be polite and try to solve the situation. When you receive positive reviews, respond with a thank you and give them a little information about what they can look forward to in the next coming weeks. For example, you might say "Thank you for your comment. I believe that our soon-to-be-announced newest product will be of interest to you. Look for our new ad in the next couple of weeks." This will keep this customer, along with any other customer who read your comment, engaged in your new ads. As you continue to work toward this goal, you will learn more about what your customers want and what makes them feel appreciated. You will be able to use this information to help keep your customers engaged.

Pay attention to your customer's language. Everyone speaks in a different way, which means they write differently. You don't want to respond to a customer in such a way that they don't understand what you are saying. In fact, this is a quick way to lose a customer. Even if they like your product, they are going to feel inadequate and too embarrassed to ask you to explain your comment in a different way. Instead, they will look elsewhere for their product or stop engaging with you, which will slowly cause them to find a different company with the same product they desire. Further, customers come from different countries. What one customer understands as retail will not be what another customer understands. For example, in some countries people negotiate what they are looking to buy. You might find customers who send you messages asking if you are willing to take a lower price for your product. Instead of getting frustrated over this comment, understand that this is a part of their culture or they want the product but probably can't afford it. While lowering the price might be out of your control, if you can you will want to consider a special deal.

Don't be afraid to admit your mistakes. You are a human just like your customers. We all make mistakes and there are times your mistakes will be noticed by your customers. This could be a misspelling of a word in a post o comment or posting an advertisement about a special sale sooner than you planned. Whatever your mistake is, your customers are going to think highly of you when you admit and apologize for your mistake. It doesn't matter where you sit on your company's social ladder. For example, Amazon CEO Jeff Bezos is known to make public apologies when someone on the Amazon team makes a mistake and people notice. For instance, when Amazon Kindle first came out many books were automatically deleted due to copyright issues. It didn't matter if a customer owned the book on their kindle, it was gone. This angered a lot of customers, who spoke publicly about refusing to use Amazon services again. Of course, the Amazon team quickly sent out a generic public apology and explained why this occurred. While some customers understood and accepted this apology many other customers did not. This is when Bezos decided to issue his own public apology. This changed the minds of a lot of customers. Many people accepted Bezos's apology and continued to use Amazon services.

7. **Keep detailed notes** on your customers and what keeps them engaged Sometimes you might try a strategy and it won't work as well as something else. While part of this will depend on your customers, another part will depend on the strategy itself. You can keep notes on anything from advertising to conversations with customers. For example, if you have a customer who is always engaging in your posts with comments or sharing, take notice. If this behavior continues for a while, take time to reach out to the customer and thank them for their efforts.

Conclusion

You now have all the information you need about creating the best Facebook business profile, how to advertise, using advertising strategies, and how to keep your customers engaged. Through the contents in this book, you will be able to take your business to the next level.

Whether you are just starting or established your business ten years ago, you will be able to grow your business with Facebook. If you haven't created your Facebook business page, this is your first step. From there, you can create advertisements following your schedule and budget. By paying attention to your customers' needs and wants, you will be able to develop some of the most engaging advertisements for your target audience.

Creating an ideal customer profile is an important step when you are determining your target audience. Through your ideal customer, you can get an idea of their age range, location, gender, and interests. Once your advertisements are up and running, you will be able to use Facebook's analytics in order to improve your ideal customer profile. This will only help you increase engagement and customers.

Once you have your ideal customer in place, you will want to create a detailed marketing plan. This plan will include everything from your mission to your customer service support.

This book is created as a guide that you can read and reread. It will be helpful as you start to grow your customer base through Facebook. You can turn to the pages of this book when you are looking for your next advertising strategy, such as PPC or Facebook Messenger Ads. If you are unsure of your next step, you can look through this book as it will help you reach your next step.

Your dedication, patience, will to succeed and this valuable information are going to take you farther than you thought possible in the Facebook advertising market. No matter how prepared you are to integrate the words of this book into your Facebook advertising, you want to remember that it all takes time. No success happens overnight. Whether your business is one year old or twenty, it will take time for Facebook users to start noticing your business and advertising. Don't let this discourage you. Instead, remember success comes to those who are patient and dedicated.

Bibliography

16 of our most powerful strategies for advertising on Facebook. (2017). Retrieved 30 July 2019, from https://adespresso.com/blog/advertising-on-facebook-strategies/

Beese, J. (2016). 10 Facebook posting tips to improve your brand awareness. Retrieved 3 August 2019, from https://sproutsocial.com/insights/facebook-posting-tips/

Dane, J. (2017). 19 Facebook ad strategies to reach your wildest goals. Retrieved 3 August 2019, from https://klientboost.com/ppc/facebook-ad-strategies/

Hassan, W. (2014). 7 benefits of using Facebook for business promotion. Retrieved 29 July 2019, from https://www.b2bmarketing.net/en/resources/blog/7-benefits-using-facebook-business-promotion

Hearn, I. (2017). Is a Facebook pay-per-click (PPC) campaign worth it in 2019? Retrieved 28 July 2019, from https://www.impactbnd.com/blog/facebook-payperclick-campaign-worth

Laja, P. (2011). How images can boost your conversion rate. Retrieved 28 July 2019 from https://conversionxl.com/blog/how-images-can-boost-your-conversion-rate/

Main, K. (2018). How to create Facebook Messenger Ads in 8 steps. Retrieved 3 August 2019, from https://fitsmallbusiness.com/facebook-messenger-ads/

Moorman, P. (2018). How to create profitable Facebook and Instagram ad campaigns. Retrieved 28 July 2019, from https://www.sourcify.com/how-to-create-profitable-facebook-and-instagram-ad-campaigns/

Parkinson, P. (n.d.). 10 (almost) effortless ways to boost Facebook engagement. Retrieved 29 July 2019, from https://www.postplanner.com/boost-facebook-engagement-infographic/

Standberry, S. (2017). How posting ads on Facebook can increase sales. Retrieved 28 July 2019, from https://www.lyfemarketing.com/blog/posting-ads-facebook/

Made in the
USA
Middletown, DE